100 YEARS OF who's who in BASEBALL

100 YEARS OF who's who in BASEBALL®

By the Staff of *Who's Who in Baseball* and Douglas B. Lyons

Foreword by Marty Appel

Guilford, Connecticut

An imprint of Rowman & Littlefield

Distributed by NATIONAL BOOK NETWORK

Special thanks to the Baseball Hall of Fame, Pete Palmer, Marty Appel, Doug Lyons, Rita Halpern, Stanley Harris, Warren Sherman, Rory Slifkin, Stuart Shea, Scott Gould, Mark Arrow, Ben Harris, and all of baseball's fans and players

British Library Cataloguing-in-Publication Information available
Library of Congress Cataloging-in-Publication Data available

ISBN 978-1-4930-1015-8

∞™ The paper used in this publication meets the minimum requirements of American National Standard for Information Sciences—Permanence of Paper for Printed Library Materials, ANSI/NISO Z39.48-1992.

CONTENTS

Foreword..vii

Introduction x

Author's Notes xi

1912—Ty Cobb, Frank "Home Run" Baker...1

1916—Ty Cobb 3

1917—Tris Speaker 5

1918—George Sisler...7

1919—Grover Cleveland Alexander...9

1920—Babe Ruth 11

1921—Babe Ruth 13

1922—Rogers Hornsby 15

1923—George Sisler...17

1924—Walter Johnson 19

1925—Dazzy Vance 21

1926—Max Carey 23

1927—Frankie Frisch 25

1928—Hack Wilson 27

1929—Generic Player 29

1930—Burleigh Grimes 31

1931—Bob Grove 33

1932—Al Simmons 35

1933—Chuck Klein 37

1934—Bill Terry 39

1935—Dizzy Dean 41

1936—Hank Greenberg...43

1937—Lou Gehrig...45

1938—Joe Medwick...47

1939—Jimmie Foxx...49

1940—Bucky Walters 51

1941—Bob Feller...53

1942—Joe DiMaggio..55

1943—Ted Williams 57

1944—Stan Musial...59

1945—Hal Newhouser, Paul Trout 61

1946—Hal Newhouser 63

1947—Eddie Dyer..65

1948—Ralph Kiner, Johnny Mize 67

1949—Lou Boudreau 69

1950—Mel Parnell 71

1951—Jim Konstanty..73

1952—Stan Musial..75

1953—Hank Sauer, Bobby Shantz 77

1954—Al Rosen 79

1955—Al Dark..81

1956—Duke Snider 83

1957—Mickey Mantle..85

1958—Warren Spahn..87

1959—Bob Turley 89

1960—Don Drysdale...91

1961—Roger Maris..93

1962—Whitey Ford 95

1963—Don Drysdale...97

1964—Sandy Koufax 99
1965—Ken Boyer, Larry Jackson, Joe Torre, Juan Marichal, Tony Oliva 101
1966—Sandy Koufax, Willie Mays, Sam McDowell, Eddie Fisher, Zoilo Versalles 103
1967—Frank Robinson, Sandy Koufax, Roberto Clemente, Jim Kaat..................................105
1968—Carl Yastrzemski 107
1969—Denny McLain, Pete Rose, Bob Gibson, Carl Yastrzemski..109
1970—Tom Seaver, Harmon Killebrew, Willie McCovey, Denny McLain, Mike Cuellar 111
1971—Johnny Bench, Jim Perry, Bob Gibson, Boog Powell...113
1972—Joe Torre, Vida Blue...115
1973—Steve Carlton, Dick Allen 117
1974—Nolan Ryan, Reggie Jackson, Pete Rose..119
1975—Lou Brock, Jeff Burroughs, Steve Garvey 121
1976—Fred Lynn, Joe Morgan 123
1977—Thurman Munson, Joe Morgan 125
1978—George Foster, Rod Carew 127
1979—Ron Guidry, Jim Rice, Dave Parker 129
1980—Willie Stargell, Keith Hernandez, Don Baylor 131
1981—George Brett, Mike Schmidt 133
1982—Fernando Valenzuela, Rollie Fingers 135
1983—Robin Yount, Dale Murphy 137
1984—Cal Ripken Jr., Ron Kittle, Darryl Strawberry...139
1985—Ryne Sandberg, Willie Hernandez 141
1986—Dwight Gooden, Don Mattingly, Willie McGee 143
1987—Roger Clemens, Mike Schmidt 145
1988—Mark McGwire, George Bell, Andre Dawson 147
1989—José Canseco, Kirk Gibson 149
1990—Robin Yount, Kevin Mitchell...151
1991—Ryne Sandberg, Cecil Fielder, Nolan Ryan..153
1992—Roger Clemens, Terry Pendleton, Cal Ripken Jr. 155
1993—Dennis Eckersley, Barry Bonds, Greg Maddux 157
1994—Barry Bonds, Frank Thomas, Jack McDowell, Greg Maddux 159
1995—Frank Thomas, Jeff Bagwell, David Cone, Greg Maddux...161
1996—Greg Maddux, Barry Larkin, Mo Vaughn, Randy Johnson 163
1997—Alex Rodriguez, John Smoltz, Pat Hentgen, Ken Caminiti...165
1998—Mark McGwire, Roger Clemens, Pedro Martinez, Larry Walker 167
1999—Mark McGwire, Sammy Sosa..169
2000—Chipper Jones, Pedro Martinez, Randy Johnson, Ivan Rodriguez 171
2001—Pedro Martinez, Jason Giambi, Jeff Kent, Randy Johnson 173
2002—Barry Bonds, Randy Johnson, Ichiro Suzuki 175
2003—Randy Johnson, Barry Bonds, Miguel Tejada...177
2004—Barry Bonds, Eric Gagne, Roy Halladay, Alex Rodriguez..179
2005—Roger Clemens, Johan Santana, Ichiro Suzuki, Barry Bonds......................................181
2006—Alex Rodriguez, Bartolo Colon, Chris Carpenter, Albert Pujols 183
2007—Johan Santana, Justin Morneau, Ryan Howard, Brandon Webb..................................185
2008—Alex Rodriguez, C.C. Sabathia, Jimmy Rollins, Jake Peavy 187
2009—Albert Pujols, Cliff Lee, Tim Lincecum, Dustin Pedroia 189
2010—Joe Mauer, Tim Lincecum, Zack Greinke, Albert Pujols..191
2011—Roy Halladay, Josh Hamilton, Joey Votto, Félix Hernandez 193
2012—Justin Verlander, Clayton Kershaw, Ryan Braun 195
2013—Miguel Cabrera, David Price, R. A. Dickey, Buster Posey..197
2014—Clayton Kershaw, Andrew McCutchen, Miguel Cabrera, Max Scherzer.........................199
2015—Mike Trout, Corey Kluber, Clayton Kershaw 201
Acknowledgments 202
About the Author 203

FOREWORD

By Marty Appel

Before baseball became a year-round, nonstop 24/7 bombardment of news, with the winter months filled with rumors, free agent signings, trades, blogs, tweets, press conferences, MLB Network, ESPN, and Tommy John surgeries—we could pause after the World Series, catch our breaths, and gently count the days until spring training.

In the really old days, people were said to sit around a "hot stove" and talk baseball, and the talk was often things like "who's better—Ruth or Cobb?!"

The first sign of spring training being just around the corner was often a sighting of a handy little publication on the corner newsstand called *Who's Who in Baseball*. Digest size, it would catch one's eye with its distinctive red cover, and the sight of it would bring joy and hope that the new season was almost here.

It first appeared in 1912 when William Howard Taft was in the White House, and as Taft was also the first president to throw out the ceremonial first pitch of the season, the coincidence seems appropriate. At a time when the president deemed it worthwhile to christen a new season, the publisher of *Baseball Magazine* deemed it a good time to give the fans a guide to all the big-league players, while getting their statistical house in order.

It likely took its name from Marquis's *Who's Who in America*, first published in the United States in 1899, and by 1912, well established as a prestigious directory of the nation's movers and shakers. To get into *Who's Who in Baseball*, one needed to be on a major league roster in 1911. To baseball fans, that was prestige enough.

Fans were probably delighted. By today's standards, it didn't offer much—games played, batting average, and fielding average were all you got, and let's face it, who has ever cared much for fielding average anyway. But you had all the players alphabetically, with their height and weight and birthdate, their full name, and of course, whether they batted or threw right- or left-handed.

It ran from Babe Adams to Heinie Zimmerman, and proudly stated in the front matter, "There is no book on the market that gives this information—it is absolutely the FIRST and ONLY BOOK OF ITS KIND."

It had a generic cover, sold for 30 cents, and probably didn't sell all that well, because *Baseball Magazine* put the idea to rest for another four years, before bringing out a 1916 edition, with Ty Cobb gracing the cover.

That 1916 edition was deemed by the publisher to really be the first edition, so that in 2015, a 100th edition was published (even if it was really the 101st).

Yes, for all the twists and turns to baseball stats, to all the movement to online presentations, to the rise and demise of *The Sporting News*'s heftier *Baseball Register*—*Who's Who in Baseball* endures.

It is comfort food for the baseball soul—always has been.

Its evolution has seen it pass through the hands of some of the legendary statisticians in the game's history. It has always been there for the avid fan, the casual fan, the sportswriters and broadcasters, the team executives, and yes, even for the players.

Baseball Magazine was only four years old when they put out that 1912 edition. The magazine continued to publish until 1957, and while it never had the cachet of "The Bible of Baseball" like *The Sporting News* did, it was appreciated by fans who enjoyed offbeat stories or character studies of players. For a big event, like the opening of Yankee Stadium, they could deliver strong issues with in-depth reporting.

The 1912 attempt at stats for fans in a handy size was a noble idea, and there was no shortage of progressive thinking at the editorial desks of the magazine at 70 Fifth Avenue in New York. In fact, in 1922, their publication of *The Baseball Cyclopedia*, edited by Ernest Lanigan, was the first 20th-century attempt at listing all players in history.

They reached outside of their offices for the 1916 edition, engaging John J. Lawres to put it together. Lawres was what we would today call a stat-geek: a sabermetrician. Baseball statistics drew people who loved sorting numbers, and Lawres, with his 1,200 pages of personal record keeping, was the man for the job. He edited the first six editions, and even had his short autobiography in each, writing: "The labor that was begun as a diversion has become little short of slavery, but I feel in my own little way that it is a pleasure to accomplish unknown a work that, in its creation, may please thousands who know neither my face, name or even existence."

Lanigan took over in 1922. Whether his tenure was brief or long is uncertain, for he was only listed for two years before the title of editor dropped from sight. But to have him associated with the book added a lot to its credibility. He is the man most responsible for the official acceptance of runs batted in as a statistic, and he later became the curator at the Baseball Hall of Fame when it opened its doors in 1939.

Remarkably, *Who's Who* did not include home runs as a category until 1940—five years after Babe Ruth's retirement. One can only imagine the editorial discussion at the *Baseball Magazine* offices after Ruth hit 60 home runs in 1927.

"Whaddya think, should we add home runs?"

"It would mean resetting the columns!"

"But we've done that before."

"Oh, everybody knows he hit 60."

"Okay, let it be."

And so the 1928 edition would give the reader games, at-bats, runs, hits, stolen bases, and average. The reader would know that Babe had seven stolen bases in 1927, but not 60 home runs. Crazy.

The introduction to the book in those days made clear that it was "devoted to the better known or more talented players of the two major leagues." In future years, that would expand, eventually causing the book to move from "saddle stitch" binding (staples) to a "perfect binding" (glue, with a spine). As baseball expanded, first in 1961–62, and then in 1969, 1977, 1993, and 1998, the book had no choice but to grow bigger and bigger. The 1962 edition was the first to exceed 500 players, and in 1969 it went over 600. Today it approaches 800. The 1952 edition had 128 pages, up from 96 the year before. In 1969, when four teams were added to the majors, the trim size of the book grew as well, up to approximately 5x8 (as it remains today), from 5x6. Photos of the players first appeared alongside their entries in 1965. For a few years in the 1970s, there was an alternate blue cover, an edition printed expressly for Scholastic Books. But red has prevailed as either the trim or the full cover for the run of the publication.

When *The Sporting News* introduced its annual *Baseball Register* in 1940, the popularity of *Who's Who* remained intact largely for its portability. Both publications listed a player's minor league years along with major league seasons, a feature that remains important and intact in *Who's Who* today. The *Register*'s last edition was published in 2007.

Clifford Bloodgood was listed as editor from 1940 to 1951, followed by Joseph Lilly and Sid Feder. Then the publication fell into the hands of Harris Publications, a family owned publisher of many magazine titles. Harris continues publication to this day.

Harris hired Allan Roth, who was also serving as the Brooklyn Dodgers' statistician, and who continued until 1973. Roth is considered one of the great statisticians in baseball history, and at the time, no teams employed anyone in such a role. He took record keeping to new levels, recognizing many of the tenets that helped give birth to the Society of American Baseball Research (SABR). Roth was a godlike figure to the early SABR people, and his connection to *Who's Who* added great credibility to the book.

In 1973, the Elias Sports Bureau took over the editorial responsibility, as Seymour Siwoff and his staff took it on for a decade. In 1983, Norman MacLean, assisted by the great sports historian Bill Shannon, assumed the editorial work, later assisted by Pete Palmer and a number of others. Palmer, also a towering figure among the stat-loving public, took full charge in 2008.

The individual player entries tended to grow as baseball changed some of its rules. When players on the disabled list were allowed to "rehab" in the minor leagues before returning to their teams, that created an extra line, even if it was only for a game or two. There would be few players—Bob Feller comes to mind—who never played in the minors, and then played their entire career in one city with one team, as Feller did with Cleveland. That "perfect entry" of his was rare.

Then there were people like Rudy Seanez, a pitcher with a lot of frequent flier mileage, who appeared for the last time in the 2008 edition. (Maybe Rudy was the reason *The Sporting News Register* shut down after 2007.) Seanez's entry took 45 lines of year-by-year stats to cover his 16 seasons, with an additional six lines for the postseason and two lines of career totals, and then came the listing of his trips to the disabled list—12—and the times he filed for free agency—also 12—plus the five times he was released and the five times he was traded. Rudy did pitch in the minor leagues in 2009, but by then, he was gone from *Who's Who*, presumably to make room for four or five additional players.

I wonder if Rudy Seanez knows about this? I wonder if he knows that along with Hank Aaron,

Derek Jeter, Jackie Robinson, and Yogi Berra, he never made a *Who's Who in Baseball* cover.

Doug Lyons has done a great job in covering the evolution of the cover subjects and taking us through baseball history over the last 100 years as well. It's a journey worth taking, and thank you *Who's Who* for still being part of our love affair with baseball.

INTRODUCTION

By Douglas B. Lyons

I have not been a baseball fan all my life. My brothers George and Jeffrey were devout fans (George: St. Louis Cardinals, Jeffrey: Boston Red Sox), but I didn't catch the baseball bug until I was 23. A friend thought I might like reading Jim Bouton's *Ball Four*.

I did and I was hooked. Since then, I have read as many baseball books as I can find. I have also written 10: three baseball trivia books with Jeffrey, two autobiographies with Red Sox broadcaster Joe Castiglione, an autobiography with the greatest pitcher of all time, softball pitcher extraordinaire Eddie Feigner of The King and His Court, an autobiography with Jim Leyritz, two baseball history/trivia books on my own, and one book of American history.

Reading about ballplayers from other eras is *not* reading ancient history. The game *then* affects the game *today*. Records are broken almost daily. Sure, the game was different, but still comparable: no African American, Latino, or Japanese players, no night games, no DH, no day games after a night game, no transcontinental travel, no air travel, no domed stadiums, no artificial turf, no closers with nasty split-fingered fastballs, not to mention lots of doubleheaders, shorter games, and a dead ball.

But talent will win out. Would Walter Johnson be a star today? Yes. What about Babe Ruth? Max Carey? Yes and yes. The ability to hit the ball consistently and to hit it hard and far is still in high demand. So is the ability to throw the ball hard or right where you want it. No other sport has the rich history of talent and characters that baseball does.

Much of American history is reflected in the history of baseball: for example, the rise of labor unions (for players and umpires), westward expansion, and integration (blacks, Hispanics, and Asians). Today, in the early part of the 21st century, a great deal of baseball research can be done on the Internet. In fact, much of it can *only* be done on a computer. Such websites as baseball-reference .com and Retrosheet.org are invaluable for the baseball researcher, or even for the casual fan who just wants to know how many home runs Mel Ott hit during his career.

Every major league team has its own website too, and many other sites are available to help the baseball researcher. The Society for American Baseball Research, founded in 1971 at Cooperstown, has an invaluable website (sabr.org), as does the National Baseball Hall of Fame (base ballhall.org). It has the largest library of baseball books, articles, and photographs extant. Many of its resources are available online.

But those are all relatively new. Statistics are kept on even the most minute aspect of the game. The entire complexion of an at-bat changes from pitch to pitch, and certainly from pitcher to pitcher and batter to batter. Is there a difference between 1-0 and 0-1? Yes! On which pitch is the runner at first more likely to break for second base? When is the best time to try a pickoff play? Is the baserunner taking a bigger lead on this pitch, and how accurate is the catcher's arm to make the long throw down to second base? But in 1912, when the first edition of *Who's Who in Baseball* was published, there was no Internet, no websites, no computers, no baseball research resources, no Hall of Fame, as we think of them today. Statistics were compiled by hand by a team of dedicated fans.

That was then, this is now. The covers of *Who's Who in Baseball* provide an overview of the history of the game. Most names and faces are familiar—Ty Cobb, Babe Ruth, Reggie Jackson, Roger Clemens, Randy Johnson. Some—Eddie Dyer, Bucky Walters, Eddie Fisher—are less so, but no less deserving. Many of the ballplayers who appeared on these covers became members of the Baseball Hall of Fame.

This book is not a complete history of baseball. But I hope you enjoy looking at the photos and reading these brief profiles of the stars of the last 100 years.

And by the way, I am not related to the Lyons of Lyons press, but I like the connection.

AUTHOR'S NOTES

The Cy Young Award

Cy Young won 511 games in his 22-year pitching career, a record that has never been approached. The Cy Young Award, emblematic of pitching excellence, was established in 1956, the year after Young died. Between 1956 and 1966, only one award was given, covering both leagues. Starting in 1967, separate awards were given for each league.

The All-Star Game

The first All-Star Game was held in Chicago on July 6, 1933, the creation of *Chicago Tribune* sports editor Arch Ward. Thirteen future Hall of Famers played. In 1945, although players were selected, no game was held because of World War II travel restrictions. Between 1959 and 1962, two All-Star Games were held each year, in an effort to raise money for the players' pension fund. Unless otherwise noted, references here are to players selected for the All-Star teams, regardless of whether they actually played in the All-Star Game.

The World Series

The "modern" World Series began in 1903, as a best-of-nine series.

No Series was held in 1904.

In 1905 the Series, now a best-of-seven affair, resumed. In 1919, the Series reverted to best-of-nine. From 1922 on, it has been a best-of-seven series. Because of a strike by the players, no Series was held in 1994.

Strikes and Lockouts

April 1–April 13, 1972. The players won the right to salary arbitration.

In 1981, the players struck for two months, from June 11 to August 10. At the end of the season, it was decided to have the first half champions play the champions of the second half.

August 12, 1994–April 2, 1995. This strike led to the unprecedented cancellation of over 900 games and the entire 1994 postseason and World Series.

The Lengthening of the Season and the Expansion of Postseason Play

Up until 1968, things were simple: There were 154 games in a season. The team with the best won-lost record in the eight-team National League met the team with the best won-lost record in the eight-team American League in the World Series, usually in late September. Except for occasional spring training games, the two teams in the Fall Classic had never faced each other or played in the opponent's ballpark—adding an exciting unknown factor to the World Series.

Those simpler days ended with expansion: In 1961 there were 10 teams in the American League. By 1962, the National League also had 10 teams. In 1961, the season was lengthened to 162 games.

Starting in 1969 each league had 12 teams and both leagues were divided into East and West divisions.

Each division had four teams. The best teams in each division met for the League Championship Series, originally a very intense best-of-five contest, the winner to go to the World Series.

In 1977, the American League went to two divisions with seven teams in each. In 1993, the NL also had 14 teams, seven in each division.

In 1994, both leagues were split into three divisions: East (five teams), West (five teams), and Central (four teams). A new twist was added, ostensibly to boost fan interest, so rooting interest wouldn't fade if your team was eliminated by August—the Wild Card.

There were now two League Division Series with four teams in each league appearing in the postseason: the three division winners plus the team in each league with the best record that was not a division winner.

There was no postseason in 1994 because of a players' strike. The first Division Series (two in each league) was instituted in 1995, a best-of-five contest. In 1998, the Milwaukee Brewers moved from the American to the National League, so both would have an even number of teams. The two winners of the ALDS and the NLDS faced each other in the League Championship Series, expanded to seven games in 1985. The winners of the NLCS and the ALCS met in the World Series.

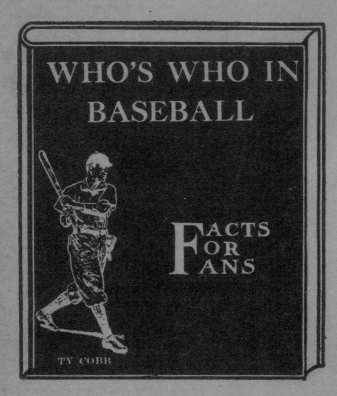

WHO'S

WHO

—IN—

BASEBALL

Price, 15 Cents

Published by the

BASEBALL MAGAZINE CO.

65 FIFTH AVE., NEW YORK

Copyrighted, 1912, by the Baseball Magazine Co., New York

1912—TY COBB, FRANK "HOME RUN" BAKER

The very first edition of *Who's Who in Baseball—Facts For Fans*, which cost 15¢, had two different covers. A white-on-black drawing of Tyrus Raymond "Ty" Cobb appears on one.

In his seventh full year with the Detroit Tigers, "The Georgia Peach" became the dominant player in the American League, which he remained for all 24 years he played. He won the AL Triple Crown in 1909.

Cobb hit in 41 straight games and led both leagues in 1911 in almost every offensive category: 147 runs scored, a batting average of .420, 127 RBIs, 83 stolen bases, 248 hits, 47 doubles, and 24 triples. He was the first winner of the AL Most Valuable Player Award and won 12 AL batting titles.

The alternate cover shows Frank "Home Run" Baker of the Philadelphia Athletics. In his 13-year Hall of Fame career, Baker, from Trappe, Maryland, was one of the slugging stars of the Dead Ball Era. He played for the A's and the New York Yankees, batting left and throwing right. His bat was a real weapon: the 5'11", 173-pound Baker swung a 52-ounce piece of lumber. (By contrast, Babe Ruth's bat weighed 46 ounces.)

Baker earned his nickname by hitting two home runs against the New York Giants in the 1911 World Series. From 1911 to 1914, he either led or tied for the league lead in home runs: 11, 10, 12, 9. He led with 130 RBIs in 1912 and 117 in 1913. He was near the top of the AL in hits, extra base hits, total bases, runs scored, doubles, and triples. Baker hit the most home runs per at-bat four times.

Baker was an outstanding third baseman too. Nine times he was either first or second in the league in putouts at the hot corner, and he led all AL third basemen in fielding percentage in 1911 and again in 1918. Six times he was either first or second in double plays turned by third basemen.

Baker's last season was 1922. He was elected to the Baseball Hall of Fame in 1955, 33 years later.

In and Around Baseball 1911

June 8: the Detroit Tigers overcome a 13–1 deficit and beat the Chicago White Sox 16–15 . . . October 24: The World Series resumes after six days of rain delays. The Philadelphia Athletics won their second consecutive World Series, beating the New York Giants 4–2.

WHO'S WHO
in BASEBALL

Price

15c

Facts
for
Fans

TY COBB

Published by the

BASEBALL MAGAZINE CO.

70 FIFTH AVENUE, NEW YORK

1916—TY COBB

The second edition of *Who's Who in Baseball—Facts for Fans*, which sold for 15¢, started the tradition of putting a picture of the outstanding player of the previous year on the cover. In 1915 Ty Cobb was in his 10th year in the major leagues. The cover has a close-up of Cobb's face.

Cobb was a master of the hands-apart batting style, moving them together just as he swung the bat. He was an excellent bunter.

The 28-year-old Cobb—although admired as a great competitor with amazing skills—did not have many friends in the game, and his racial attitudes, more mainstream then, would be decried today. He had one of the best seasons any player ever had in 1915, leading the American League in batting (.369), hits (208), singles (161), runs (144), total bases (274), and stolen bases (96, an AL record which stood for 47 years until broken by Maury Wills with 104 in 1972).

Cobb was on base a league-leading 336 times. He also turned a league-leading eight double plays from center field. Cobb's 1915 salary was reported to be $20,000. Despite Cobb's outstanding efforts, the Tigers finished second in the AL, 2½ games behind the champion Boston Red Sox.

As good as Cobb's performance was in 1915, it was not even one of Cobb's best seasons: he won the Triple Crown in 1909, leading the AL in batting (.377), home runs (9!), and RBIs (107). He was the AL's first Most Valuable Player in 1911,

batting .420. In 1912, he hit .409. In 1922, at the age of 35, he still managed to hit .401.

In 1927, after 22 years with the Tigers, he went to the Philadelphia Athletics for the final two years of his playing career. His career hit record, 4,189, stood for 57 years, until eclipsed on September 11, 1985 by Pete Rose, who retired with 4,256 hits.

Between 1907 and 1919, Cobb led the AL in batting for an unmatched 12 seasons. He hit over .400 three times and retired with a career batting average of .366.

While still a player, Cobb managed the Detroit Tigers for six seasons (1921–1926).

In 1936, Cobb was one of the first five players elected to the Baseball Hall of Fame along with Babe Ruth, Honus Wagner, Christy Mathewson, and Walter Johnson. These five all-time greats are represented by the five stars in the Hall of Fame's logo.

Cobb became one of the richest men in baseball thanks to early investments in a growing Atlanta soda company (Coca-Cola) and a growing car company (United Motors, which later merged with General Motors).

In and Around Baseball 1915:

The Boston Red Sox beat the Philadelphia Phillies 4–1 in the World Series, the last postseason appearance by the Phillies until 1950.

WHO'S WHO in BASEBALL

FACTS
FOR
FANS

PRICE
15c.

TRIS SPEAKER

Published by the

BASEBALL MAGAZINE CO.
70 FIFTH AVENUE, NEW YORK
Copyrighted, 1917, by the Baseball Magazine Co.
New York

1917—TRIS SPEAKER

This cover was a new format for *Who's Who in Baseball*: the background was thick red and white stripes. Tris Speaker, "The Grey Eagle," a native of Hubbard, Texas, is considered one of the greatest outfielders and greatest players in history. He revolutionized center field play by playing very shallow, challenging batters to hit the ball over his head. Few did because Speaker's blazing speed combined with his strong and accurate arm turned many long flyballs into outs. Speaker patrolled the outfield for 22 seasons, starting with the Boston Americans (later the Red Sox) in 1907. He went on to play for the Cleveland Indians (1916–1926), and briefly the Washington Senators and Philadelphia Athletics.

Speaker was a natural righty, but taught himself to throw left-handed when his right arm was broken twice after being thrown by a horse. Then he turned to batting lefty too.

In 1912, Speaker was the American League's second MVP and led the AL in home runs with 10. He scored over 100 runs in seven seasons. Thirteen times Speaker hit more than 10 triples in a season.

Speaker also holds the major league record for double plays by an outfielder (139) and assists by an outfielder (449). Eighty-six years after he retired in 1928, he still holds the AL mark for putouts by an outfielder (6,788), exceeded only by Willie Mays's National League mark of 7,095.

Speaker was insulted when Red Sox management tried to cut his salary after the 1915 season because his batting average slipped from .338 to .322, and he would not sign with Boston for 1916. He was traded to the Cleveland Indians, and in 1916 Speaker had a .386 batting average, 211 hits, a .470 on-base percentage, and a .502 slugging percentage, tops in the majors. He also led the AL with 41 doubles, one of eight times he led the league in two-baggers. Speaker's 87-year-old career record for doubles—792—may stand forever. It's 46 ahead of his closest challenger, Pete Rose. But the Indians finished 1916 in seventh place (in an eight-team league), 77-77.

Speaker was a player-manager for the Cleveland Indians from 1919 to 1926, winning the World Series in 1920, a 5–2 victory over the Brooklyn Robins (later the Dodgers) in the best-of-nine series.

He retired with a career batting average of .345. Speaker was elected to the Baseball Hall of Fame in 1937, the seventh man elected.

In and Around Baseball 1916:

September 8: Wally Schang of the Philadelphia Athletics is the first player to hit a home run from both sides of the plate in one game. The A's win that game but still finish with an all-time worst record of 36-117.

The Boston Red Sox beat the Brooklyn Robins 4–1 in the World Series.

WHO'S WHO
in BASEBALL

GEORGE SISLER

FACTS
FOR
FANS

PRICE
15c.

Published BASEBALL MAGAZINE CO. 70 FIFTH AVE. NEW YORK
by the
Copyright, 1918, by The Baseball Magazine Co., N.Y.

1918—GEORGE SISLER

"Gorgeous" George Sisler's 1917 statistics were outstanding: second in batting (.353), second in hits (190), third in singles (149), first in double plays turned at first base (97), fourth in total bases (244), fourth in doubles (30), and fifth in stolen bases (37). But his St. Louis Browns, a perennially dreadful team, finished seventh in a league of eight. Only the Philadelphia Athletics were worse.

After graduating from the University of Michigan with a degree in mechanical engineering, Sisler spent 15 years in the major leagues with the St. Louis Browns (1915–1927), then was briefly with the Washington Senators, and finished his career with the Boston Braves (1928–1930). Although he started out as a pitcher (24 games, 5 wins, 6 losses), the 5'11", 170-pound Sisler spent most of his career as a first baseman—one of the greatest. He led the American League in assists for a first baseman for six seasons.

Swinging a 42-ounce bat, Sisler was the AL batting champ in 1920 (.407) and 1922 (.420), and was the AL Most Valuable Player in 1922. His career batting average was .340. On March 30, 1925, he became the first baseball player to appear on the cover of *Time* magazine.

Sisler is one of the few players who had two sons play in the majors—Dave and Dick. Dick was an All-Star in 1950. A third son, George Jr., went on to become president of the International League.

Sisler was elected to the Hall of Fame in 1939.

In and Around Baseball 1917:

May 2: Pitcher Fred Toney of the Cincinnati Reds faces Hippo Vaughn, pitching for the Cubs in Chicago. Each throws a no-hitter for nine innings. Toney wins 1–0 in 10 innings . . . June 23: Boston Red Sox starting pitcher Babe Ruth walks Ray Morgan of the Washington Senators on four straight balls. After arguing with home plate umpire Clarence "Brick" Owens, Ruth is ejected. Ernie Shore comes on in relief. New catcher Sam Agnew throws Morgan out trying to steal. Shore then retires the next 26 batters—for a very unusual combined no-hitter.

The Chicago White Sox beat the New York Giants 4–2 in the World Series.

WHO'S WHO in BASEBALL

FACTS FOR FANS

PRICE 15c.

GROVER CLEVELAND ALEXANDER

Published by the BASEBALL MAGAZINE CO. 70 FIFTH AVE. NEW YORK

1919—GROVER CLEVELAND ALEXANDER

Grover Cleveland "Old Pete" Alexander, one of 13 children, was named for the 22nd and 24th president of the United States. In the 1952 film *The Winning Team*, he was played by Ronald Reagan, the 40th president. Alexander is the only major leaguer born in Elba, Nebraska. He pitched for the Philadelphia Phillies, Chicago Cubs, and St. Louis Cardinals. His career won-loss record was 373-208.

In 1911, his rookie season, Alexander led the majors with 28 wins and seven shutouts. In 367 innings, he faced 1,440 batters, also league-leading numbers.

Alexander missed most of the 1918 season while serving in the US Army as a sergeant with the 342nd Field Artillery Unit in France during World War I. (He is pictured wearing his army uniform.) He pitched just three games for the Cubs, going 2-1. Artillery fire cost him most of the hearing in his right ear (which was later amputated), and brought on epileptic seizures. He also became an alcoholic. Alexander is the only player who appeared on the cover of *Who's Who in Baseball* after playing only three games the previous season.

No pitcher in the history of the National League has won more games. When Alexander retired in 1930, he thought his 373 wins were the most in NL history—one more than his rival Christy Mathewson. Later research gave Mathewson one more victory, leaving them tied.

Alexander won the Triple Crown of Pitching three times. In 1915, he was 31-10, with 241 strikeouts and a 1.22 ERA for the Phillies. In 1916 with the Phils he won 33 games, whiffed 167, and had an ERA of just 1.55. In 1920, this time with the Cubs, he had 27 wins, 173 strikeouts, and a 1.91 ERA. Through 2014, the only other National Leaguer who has won the Triple Crown of Pitching three times is Sandy Koufax, who did it for the Los Angeles Dodgers in 1963, 1965, and 1966.

In addition to leading the National League in ERA in the three years he won the Triple Crown of Pitching, he also had the lowest ERA in the NL in 1919, and finished his career with an ERA of 2.56 over 5,190 innings and 436 complete games—truly staggering numbers.

Alexander led the National League in wins in six seasons. In five seasons he had the fewest walks per nine innings. For six years, he was either first or second in the league in strikeouts per nine innings. He led the NL in innings pitched seven times and in strikeouts six.

Alexander was a speedy workhorse, frequently pitching a complete game in under 90 minutes. He led the league in wins and complete games for six seasons, including four in a row (1914–1917), and seven times in shutouts.

Alexander pitched all nine innings in Game 2 of the 1926 World Series for the St. Louis Cardinals, to beat the New York Yankees in under two hours. Seven days later, Alexander also won Game 6, another complete game.

The next day, in Game 7, he was probably sleeping in the St. Louis bullpen in the top of the seventh inning when the Cardinals' starter, future Hall of Famer Jesse Haines, developed a blister on his pitching hand. The Cardinals were leading 3–2, but with two outs, the bases were loaded with Yankees: Earle Combs was on third, Bob Meusel on second, and Lou Gehrig on first. With Tony Lazzeri, another future Hall of Famer coming up to bat, Cardinals' player/manager Rogers Hornsby signaled to the bullpen. Alexander, then 39 years old, woke up, walked in, and pitched. He struck out Lazzeri—one of the most dramatic moments in baseball history. The Yankees went down 1-2-3 in the eighth.

In the bottom of the ninth, Babe Ruth walked, but inexplicably tried to steal second base. He was thrown out by Cardinals catcher Bob O'Farrell for the final out of the game and the Series: two plays which will live forever in baseball lore in consecutive innings. The Cardinals won the Series 4 games to 3.

In 1930, his final season, at 43 he was the oldest player in the National League. Alexander was elected to the Hall of Fame in 1938.

In and Around Baseball 1918:

For the only time since 1885, no grand slams were hit in the American League all season . . . James "Hippo" Vaughn of the Chicago Cubs wins the National League Triple Crown of Pitching, leading the NL with 22 wins, 148 strikeouts, and an ERA of 1.74.

The 1918 World Series was the last world championship for the Boston Red Sox for 86 years. They beat the Cubs 4–2 but didn't win again until their historic victory in 2004. 🢒

WHO'S WHO in BASEBALL

ACCURATE
and
COMPLETE
RECORDS
for
EVERY YEAR
—
Price 25c

EVERY STAR
PLAYER
in
BASEBALL
—

BABE RUTH

Published
by the **BASEBALL MAGAZINE CO.** 70 FIFTH AVE.
NEW YORK

Copyrighted 1920 by the Baseball Magazine Co., N. Y.

1920—BABE RUTH

George Herman "Babe" Ruth spent his sixth and last year with the Boston Red Sox in 1919. He had a pretty good year on the mound (17 games, 9-5, with an ERA of 2.97), but his numbers at the plate were gargantuan—like Ruth himself.

Ruth led both leagues with 103 runs scored, the first of eight times Ruth led the American League in this category. He hit 29 home runs—more than the Chicago White Sox, Cleveland Indians, Detroit Tigers, and Washington Senators, and more than the total Ruth himself had hit in his previous five seasons *combined*. His three closest competitors in the AL were teammate Frank "Home Run" Baker, Tillie Walker of the Philadelphia Athletics, and George Sisler of the St. Louis Browns. Each had 10 home runs. (Amazingly, *Who's Who in Baseball* did not list home runs until 1940.)

Ruth led both leagues with 113 RBIs. His on-base percentage was .456—tops in the majors. He led both leagues with 284 total bases. His batting average was "only" .322, #7 behind Ty Cobb's .384. Ruth's slugging percentage of .657 not only led the AL, it was over *100* points higher than that of his closest rival, George Sisler's .530. This was the second of 13 times Ruth led the AL in slugging percentage.

Ruth hit a home run once every 14.9 at-bats. His next closest competitor was the Indians' Elmer Smith, who homered once every 43.9 at-bats.

While 1919 was not Ruth's last year as a pitcher, he never again pitched more than two games in a single season, and even then, never more than nine innings in any one year. The reason is obvious: A starting pitcher can work only once every four or five days. But an outfielder can play the field and bat *every* day. And no matter how good a pitcher Ruth was, he was certainly a better batter. His hitting—especially his *power* hitting—signaled the end of the Dead Ball Era and changed the game forever. Home runs were no longer considered vulgar.

The Black Sox scandal occurred in 1919, although the nefarious deeds of eight members of the Chicago White Sox in "fixing" the 1919 World Series were not revealed until December 1919, by Chicago sportswriter Hugh Fullerton and others. The scandal remains the biggest black eye in baseball's long history, because it went right to the heart and integrity of the game: Fans have the right to believe that each player is trying his hardest to win the game. Gambling on the game—the reason the 1919 Series was thrown—is still considered the worst sin in baseball.

Ruth's accomplishments at the plate—his home runs, prodigious not only in how far he hit them, but how many and how often—drew the public's attention away from the tawdry side of the game. He brought many disillusioned fans back to the ballpark. (Yankees' attendance in 1919: 619,164. In 1920: 1,289,422.)

Ruth's Hall of Fame plaque notes that he was the game's biggest drawing card.

In and Around Baseball 1919:

August 24: Cleveland Indians pitcher Ray Caldwell is struck by lightning during a game. He finishes it and wins 2–1 . . . Shocking. September 28: In the first game of a doubleheader, the New York Giants beat the Philadelphia Phillies 6–1 in 51 minutes—the shortest game ever.

The 1919 World Series matched the Chicago White Sox with the Cincinnati Reds. Unbeknownst to all but a few, eight members of the White Sox either took money to throw the Series, or knew that their teammates were doing so and did nothing. The Reds won the best-of-nine series 5–3. Following the disclosure of the "Black Sox Scandal," baseball commissioner Kenesaw Mountain Landis banned eight members of the White Sox forever, despite their acquittal at trial: Joe Jackson (whose swing Babe Ruth tried to copy), Eddie Cicotte, Arnold "Chick" Gandil, Oscar "Happy" Felsch, Fred McMullin, Charles "Swede" Risberg, George "Buck" Weaver, and Claude Williams.

Complete
Records
of Every
Star
Player
for
Every
Year

WHO'S WHO IN BASEBALL

Including

Life Story

of

BABE RUTH

Pub by
*Baseball
Magazine*
Co., N. Y.

Price 25c

1921—BABE RUTH

During his six years with the Boston Red Sox, George Herman "Babe" Ruth was one of the greatest pitchers in the game (89 wins, 46 losses, with an ERA of 2.19). But he could hit too. And he had power—enough power to revolutionize the game. "The Sultan of Swat" was the first player to appear on the cover of Who's Who in Baseball in consecutive seasons.

On December 26, 1919, the Red Sox, short of cash, sold Ruth to the New York Yankees for $125,000—a fortune at the time. Ruth had led the Red Sox to World Series victories in 1915, 1916, and 1918—their last world championship until 2004, thanks to the "Curse of the Bambino."

Once he arrived in New York, a bigger city with a bigger stage for Ruth's enormous personality—he did everything big—the Yankees changed. Ruth had hit 11 home runs for Boston in 1918 and 29 in 1919. But his home run total exploded in 1920: 54 home runs, 35 more than his closest competitor, George Sisler of the St. Louis Browns. His 54 home runs were more than any team in the American League besides his new team, the Yankees. The other seven teams averaged 46 home runs for the season. His home run total was also more than every team in the National League except the Philadelphia Phillies, who hit 64. He hit a home run once every 8.5 at-bats. Once again his closest competitor was Sisler, who homered once every 33.2 at-bats. Ruth also led the major leagues with 135 RBIs and 158 runs scored, 55 more than he had scored the previous season.

In 1920, Ruth led the American League with 150 walks— the first of 11 years he would lead the league in that category. He did not win the Triple Crown because he batted only .376, behind George Sisler's .407, Tris Speaker's .388, and Joe Jackson's .382. Ruth was tops in the AL with 99 extra base hits and was on base 325 times, nine more than Tris Speaker.

Although the Yankees won 15 more games (95) than in 1919 (80), they finished in third place again, three games behind the pennant-winning Cleveland Indians.

In and Around Baseball 1920:

April 16: A pitch thrown by the Yankees' submarine-style pitcher Carl Mays hit Ray Chapman of the Cleveland Indians in the head. He died the next day—major league baseball's only on-field player fatality . . . Major League Baseball outlaws the spitball and other "freak" pitches that involve defacing the ball, or putting a foreign substance on it. The 17 pitchers still throwing the spitball are allowed to finish their careers with it . . . October 2: For the only time in major league history, there's a tripleheader: the Pirates play the Cincinnati Reds in Pittsburgh. They lose the first two and win the last . . . The Philadelphia Phillies manage only 283 walks, still the lowest season-total ever.

Something happened in Game 5 of the 1920 World Series between the Cleveland Indians and the Brooklyn Robins (Dodgers) which hadn't happened before, and hasn't happened since: In the top of the fifth inning at Cleveland's Dunn Field, Cleveland's Bill Wambsganss turned an unassisted triple play—in his hometown! Cleveland beat Brooklyn 5–2 in the best-of-nine contest. Not enough excitement? That was the first World Series game in which a pitcher (the Indians' Jim Bagby) hit a home run. And it saw the first World Series grand slam, by Elmer Smith of the Indians.

Rogers
Hornsby
Baseball's
Champion
Batter
1921

WHO'S
WHO
IN
BASEBALL

*Complete
Life Records
of more than
200
Major League
Players*

A SPECIAL FEATURE
*Striking Events
of the 1921
Baseball Season*

Published by the
**BASEBALL
MAGAZINE**
*70 Fifth Ave.
New York City*

Price 25c.

1922—ROGERS HORNSBY

In 1921, Rogers Hornsby—"The Rajah," from Winters, Texas—played in all 154 games for the St. Louis Cardinals, mostly at second base, with 235 hits, a .397 batting average, 378 total bases, 131 runs scored, 126 RBIs, 83 extra base hits, 44 doubles, 18 triples, 302 times on base, a slugging percentage of .639, and an on-base percentage of .458—a truly monster season.

Hornsby would have won the Triple Crown (which he won in both 1922 and in 1925), but he hit "only" 21 home runs, second to the 23 hit by George "High Pockets" Kelly.

Hornsby broke in to the majors at 19 with the St. Louis Cardinals—the start of a 23-year playing career. He was a player-manager for 15 of those years, leading the St. Louis Cardinals to their first world championship in 1926.

Hornsby is recognized as the greatest right-handed batter in history. His career average was .358, the highest in National League history. Hornsby won the batting title seven times, including six in a row (1920–1925) and hit over .400 three times, including a 20th-century record of .424 in 1924. He won the NL MVP in 1925 and 1929. In 1924, he became the first National Leaguer to hit his 300th career home run.

In 1922, Hornsby became the first National Leaguer to hit 40 home runs in a single season. He hit 42.

He didn't go to the movies or read newspapers for fear that he'd strain his eyes. Asked what he did during the winter, Hornsby said he gazed out the window and waited for spring.

He was elected to the Baseball Hall of Fame in 1942. The St. Louis Cardinals would have retired Hornsby's uniform number, but he played before numbers were worn. A Cardinals logo with his initials hangs at Busch Stadium.

In and Around Baseball 1921:

January 12: Federal Judge Kenesaw Mountain Landis becomes the first commissioner of baseball . . . July 18: Babe Ruth of the New York Yankees hits career home run #139, and becomes career home run leader, passing Roger Connor . . . August 5: With Harold Arlin behind the KDKA microphone, baseball is broadcast for the first time on the radio. Final score: Pittsburgh Pirates 8, Philadelphia Phillies 5.

The 1921 World Series is the first broadcast on the radio. For the first time ever, all games in the 1921 World Series are played in the same ballpark—New York City's Polo Grounds, where the Giants and the Yankees both play. The Giants won 5–3 in the best-of-nine series.

WHO'S WHO IN BASEBALL

Complete Life Records of more than 200 Major League Players

George Sisler
Baseball's Champion Batter For 1922

Copyrighted by the
BASEBALL MAGAZINE
COMPANY 1923

Price 25c.

1923—GEORGE SISLER

George Sisler was the third player to appear twice on the cover of *Who's Who in Baseball*, after Ty Cobb and Babe Ruth. In 1922 he hit .420 to win the American League batting title and also led with 134 runs scored, 246 hits, 18 triples, and 51 stolen bases. Sisler hit in 41 consecutive games and was the AL Most Valuable Player. But his St. Louis Browns finished the 1922 season just one game behind the pennant-winning New York Yankees.

1922 was Sisler's second season hitting over .400. In 1920, he led the majors with .407. He hit over .300 for 14 of his 15 years in the majors. His 1920 record of 257 hits stood for 84 years until Seattle's Ichiro Suzuki broke it with 262 in 2004.

Sisler missed the entire 1923 season when a sinusitis infection led to headaches and double vision. He went on to manage the Browns.

His speech at the Hall of Fame's first induction ceremony in 1939 is one of the shortest on record—just three sentences.

In and Around Baseball 1922:

May 20: Babe Ruth is named captain of the New York Yankees. After he climbed into the stands to fight with a heckler on May 25, Ruth was replaced as captain by shortstop Everett Scott . . . August 7: Ken Williams of the St. Louis Browns becomes the first major leaguer in the 20th century to homer twice in one inning . . . August 30: Charlie Robertson of the Chicago White Sox pitches a perfect game against the Tigers at Navin Field in Detroit . . . Rogers Hornsby wins the Triple Crown and becomes the only man to hit at least 40 home runs (he hit 42), and bat over .400 (he hit .401) in the same season.

For the second straight year, the Giants meet the Yankees in the World Series at the Polo Grounds. After 10 innings, Game 2 ended in a 3–3 tie because of darkness. The Giants won in a 4–0 sweep, as the World Series returned to a best-of-seven format.

WHO'S WHO IN BASEBALL

Complete Life Records of More Than 200 Major League Ball Players

Ninth Edition, 1924

Price, 25c

Walter Johnson
Premier Pitcher
of Professional
Baseball

1924—WALTER JOHNSON

In its 9th edition, Walter Johnson—nicknamed "The Big Train" and "Barney"—for Barney Oldfield, a famous race-car driver of the day—was the first pitcher to appear on the cover of *Who's Who in Baseball*.

Pitching for the Senators in 1923, a fourth place club, the 35-year-old Johnson used a unique sidearm sweep to lead the American League with 130 strikeouts, one of 12 times he led the AL in that category. In 1923, Johnson became the first pitcher to be voted AL Most Valuable Player. Radar guns were not yet available to accurately measure the speed of Johnson's pitches, but players from his era agree that his sidearm delivery gave him one of the best fastballs of all time.

Johnson spent his entire 21-year career pitching for the Washington Senators. He managed the Senators from 1929 to 1932 and then the Cleveland Indians from 1933 to 1935.

Any year you lead the league in strikeouts is a good year, but 1923 was certainly not Johnson's best season. He won the Triple Crown of Pitching in 1913, 1918, and 1924—the only American Leaguer ever to win it three times, and one of only three pitchers ever to win it three times: the others, both National Leaguers, are Grover Cleveland Alexander and Sandy Koufax. Johnson's 417 career wins is second only to Cy Young's 511 and is 44 ahead of his nearest challengers, Grover Alexander and Christy Mathewson, tied at 373. Johnson's 417 wins has been the AL record for 88 years—since Johnson retired in 1927. The only pitcher close to that is Roger Clemens, who trails by 63!

Johnson's AL record of 3,509 career strikeouts stood for 74 years until broken by Clemens, then with the Yankees, on April 3, 2001. Eighty-eight years after he retired, Johnson still holds the record for most shutouts in a career—110, 20 more than his closest rival, Grover Alexander.

In 1936 Walter Johnson was one of the first five players elected to the Baseball Hall of Fame. His induction speech was just the way he pitched: fast—just three sentences, one of which was "Thank you."

In and Around Baseball 1923:

April 18: New York slugger Babe Ruth hits the first home run at the Yankees' new home, Yankee Stadium, to beat his former team, the Boston Red Sox 4–1. The stadium was built with a short porch in right field, to take advantage of Ruth's left-handed hitting prowess—hence its nickname, "The House that Ruth Built" . . . July 22: Walter Johnson strikes out his 3,000th batter.

For an unprecedented third straight year, the Giants and the Yankees meet in the World Series. Two differences this time from the previous two years: Games 1, 3, and 5 are played in the Yankees new home, Yankee Stadium. Also, the Yankees won their first World Series, 4–2. In a unique baseball occurrence, Emil "Irish" Meusel (Giants) faces his brother Bob (Yankees) in the World Series in the same city three years in a row.

WHO'S WHO IN BASEBALL

Complete Life Records of More Than 200
Major League Ball Players

Price
25c

Tenth Edition
1925

"Dazzy"
Vance

1925—DAZZY VANCE

Charles Arthur "Dazzy" Vance, from Orient, Iowa, got his nickname as the leader of the "Daffiness Boys," an unruly group on the Brooklyn Robins (Dodgers) of the 1930s.

Vance made his major league debut at age 24 with the Pittsburgh Pirates in 1915, spent two seasons with the Yankees, but pitched his first full season in the majors and won his first big-league game at age 31 in 1922. That year, Vance became the first rookie to lead the league in strikeouts, with 134. Vance spent most of his career—12 seasons—with Brooklyn. He pitched a no-hitter against the Philadelphia Phillies on September 13, 1925.

In 1924 Vance won the National League Triple Crown of Pitching; most wins—28 with only six losses; most strikeouts—262; and lowest ERA—2.16. With his excellent fastball and outstanding curve, he also led the majors with 30 complete games, four shutouts, and 7.648 strikeouts per nine innings.

Vance was the first pitcher to be voted NL Most Valuable Player. As a reward, he was given $1,000 (in 2015, about $19,000) in gold coins!

His specialty was strikeouts. 1924 was the third of seven consecutive seasons in which he led the league in strikeouts—the only pitcher ever to do that—averaging over 191 Ks per season during that stretch. (He averaged 176 strikeouts per season his entire career.) Although he led the Dodgers to a 92-win season, they finished in second place, 1½ games behind their crosstown rivals, the Giants, who won 93.

He later pitched briefly for the Cincinnati Reds and the St. Louis Cardinals. Vance never got to the World Series with Brooklyn, but pitched briefly in one World Series game for the Cardinals in 1934.

Vance was elected to the Baseball Hall of Fame in 1955.

In and Around Baseball 1924:

Babe Ruth wins his only batting title, hitting .378 . . . Walter Johnson of the Washington Senators wins the Triple Crown of Pitching in the American League with 23 wins, 158 strikeouts, and an ERA of 2.72. It will be another 87 years before the next time there are winners of the Triple Crown of Pitching in both leagues . . . Rogers Hornsby bats .424, the highest in the modern history of the National League, and wins his fifth of six straight batting crowns . . . The Chicago Cubs are caught stealing 149 times, a modern single-season record.

"*First* in war, *first* in peace, and *LAST* in the American League"—the Washington Senators. Not in 1924. Walter Johnson won Game 7 as the Senators beat the New York Giants 4–3 in the World Series—their only world championship.

WHO'S WHO IN BASEBALL

Complete Life Records of More Than 200 Major League Ball Players

Price
25c

Eleventh Edition
1926

Max
Carey

1926—MAX CAREY

Max "Scoops" Carey (born Maximillian George Carnarius) was a switch-hitting leadoff batter for 20 years, 17 for the Pittsburgh Pirates and four for the Brooklyn Robins (Dodgers).

In 1925 he hit 343 and led the National League in stolen bases with 46. He had 39 doubles and 13 triples. He led the NL in swipes for 10 seasons and stole more than 40 bases nine times.

He hit over .300 six times. Over his career, Carey walked (1,040) more than he struck out (695). Carey was also an excellent center fielder, leading the NL in putouts seven times and assists six. Eighty-six years after his final game in 1929, he still holds the NL career record for most outfield assists—339.

He appeared in the World Series for the Pirates in 1925, hitting .458.

Following his playing career, he managed the Brooklyn Dodgers and in the All-American Girls Professional Baseball League. Carey was elected to the Baseball Hall of Fame in 1961.

In and Around Baseball 1925:

George Sisler of the St. Louis Browns starts off the season by hitting safely in 34 straight games—the longest streak ever from the start of a season . . . Walter Johnson, the Washington Senators star pitcher, bats .433—the highest ever for a pitcher with at least 50 at-bats.

Although the Washington Senators repeated as American League champions, they lost the World Series 4–3 to the Pittsburgh Pirates.

WHO'S WHO IN BASEBALL

RECORDS OF MORE THAN 200 MAJOR LEAGUE PLAYERS

Twelfth Edition

1927

Frank Frisch at Bat

Price 25c

1927—FRANKIE FRISCH

Frankie Frisch, "The Fordham Flash," went right from captaining the baseball, football, and basketball teams at Fordham University to the major leagues, where he spent the first 11 years of his big-league career (exactly 1,000 games) playing an outstanding second base for his hometown New York Giants. He then spent eight years as a St. Louis Cardinal.

In 1926, Frisch was third in stolen bases, but did not lead the National League in any major category. Hazen "Kiki" Cuyler of the Pittsburgh Pirates might have made the cover of *Who's Who in Baseball*. He topped the league with 157 games played, 113 runs scored, 35 stolen bases, 256 times on base, was second in being hit by a pitch (9), and third in the league with 143 singles.

Frisch, a switch hitter, retired as a career .316 hitter. He hit over .300 for 11 straight years. He was among the top three base stealers in the National League 10 times, leading in three of those years. He led the league in at-bats per strikeout in four seasons. Only twice did he strike out more than 20 times. Seventy-eight years after he retired, Frisch still holds the record for most assists in a season by a second baseman: 641, which he set in 1927 with the Cardinals. He was voted the National League's MVP in 1931 when the Cardinals won the pennant.

Frisch played on eight pennant winners and in 50 World Series games, and was the player/manager for the Cardinals—known as the "Gas House Gang" because of their filthy uniforms—leading them to a world championship in 1934. He also managed the Pittsburgh Pirates and the Chicago Cubs.

On August 19, 1941, it was raining at Ebbets Field in Brooklyn. Frisch, managing the Pirates, thought the game ought to be called. When he went out on the field to "discuss" it with the umpires, he brought an umbrella to emphasize his point. Umpire Jocko Conlan ejected him.

Frisch was elected to the Baseball Hall of Fame in 1947. He was killed in a car crash in 1973 in Wilmington, Delaware, on his way home from a meeting of the Hall of Fame Veterans Committee.

In and Around Baseball 1926:

Fred "Firpo" Marberry of the Washington Senators becomes the first relief pitcher with at least 20 saves in a season. He saved 22 . . . The name of the Chicago Cubs home park is changed from Weeghman Park to Wrigley Field, when the Wrigley family buys the Cubs . . . The stadium opened in 1914 as the home of the Chi-Feds of the Federal League.

World Series, Game 4, Yankees vs. St. Louis Cardinals: Babe Ruth becomes the first player to hit three home runs in a World Series game, but the Cardinals won the Series 4–3.

WHO'S WHO
IN BASEBALL
1928

THIRTEENTH EDITION

RECORDS OF MORE
THAN 200 MAJOR
LEAGUE PLAYERS

LEADING EVENTS
PAST SEASON

"HACK"
WILSON
AT BAT

PRICE
25c

1928—HACK WILSON

Lewis "Hack" Wilson got his unusual nickname because he was said to resemble popular weight-lifter and wrestler George Hackenschmidt. Wilson, 5'6", from Ellwood City, Pennsylvania, was one of the game's strangest physical specimens: size 6 shoes, size 19 neck.

In 1927, playing for the Chicago Cubs, Wilson batted .318 and led the National League with 30 home runs—his second of three straight NL home run titles. He also led with 70 strikeouts, 72 extra base hits, and 400 putouts in center field. His 129 RBIs was second in the league. But the Cubs finished fourth.

In 1930, Wilson had what is now called "a career year": he hit 56 home runs (the NL record for 68 years) and 191 RBIs—after 85 years, *still* the major league record. Things fell off for Wilson in 1931: he hit only .261 with 13 home runs and 61 RBIs, an incredible 130 fewer than in 1930.

During his 12-year career with the Giants, Cubs, Dodgers, and Phillies, he batted .307.

Wilson died at 48 in 1948 and was elected to the Baseball Hall of Fame in 1979.

It might have been Babe Ruth on the cover of *Who's Who in Baseball* in 1928. His 1927 season was historic. Not only did Ruth lead the Yankees to a 4–0 World Series sweep of the Pittsburgh Pirates, he set the modern major league record by hitting an astonishing *60* home runs—a number previously unimaginable, and a record that stood for 34 years. He homered once every nine at-bats. Ruth led the majors with 158 runs scored, 137 walks, an on-base percentage of .486, and a .772 slugging percentage. He also led the majors with 380 total bases. His batting average was .356.

In 1927, in addition to his staggering 60 home runs, Ruth drove in 165 runs, scored 158, had 192 hits, 97 extra base hits, and walked 137 times. His 1927 Yankees (including future Hall of Famers Lou Gehrig, Tony Lazzeri, Waite Hoyt, Herb Pennock, and Earle Combs) with a record of 110-44, are considered one of the best teams of all time.

In and Around Baseball 1927:

June 19: Jack Scott of the Philadelphia Phillies becomes the last major league pitcher to start—and finish—both games of a doubleheader . . . July 18: Ty Cobb of the Philadelphia Athletics get his 4,000th hit . . . The Yankees win 21 of 22 games against the St. Louis Browns . . . The Chicago Cubs become the first team to draw over one million fans.

The mighty Yankees swept the Pittsburgh Pirates in the World Series.

WHO'S WHO IN BASEBALL

Complete Life Records of More Than 200
Major League Ball Players

1929

FOURTEENTH EDITION

LEADING EVENTS PAST SEASON

PRICE
25c

Copyrighted by the BASEBALL MAGAZINE CO., 1929

1929—GENERIC PLAYER

For the first time, in 1929 the player depicted on the cover of *Who's Who in Baseball* was not a future member of Baseball's Hall of Fame. There's a generic catcher on the cover of the 1929 edition of *Who's Who in Baseball—Complete Life Records of More Than 200 Major League Ball Players*, which sold for 25¢.

Babe Ruth might have won the MVP Award in 1929, with his league-leading 46 homers, .345 batting average, and 154 RBIs. Al Simmons had the most total bases (373), the most RBIs (157), and the most extra base hits (84). But Ruth was ineligible because he had won once before, in 1923. That rule was later changed.

Dale Alexander and Charlie Gehringer ("The Mechanical Man") tied for the most hits in the league (215), and Gehringer led in triples (19).

In and Around Baseball 1928:

July 5: New York's Polo Grounds, home of the New York Giants, is the first major league stadium to install an electric public address system . . . Ty Cobb and Tris Speaker both finish their careers with the Philadelphia Athletics, #1 and #2 all time in hits: Cobb with 4,189, Speaker with 3,514 . . . The Boston Braves play nine straight doubleheaders in September . . . The American League bans the "quick pitch."

The New York Yankees, winners of 101 games, beat the St. Louis Cardinals in the World Series 4–0.

WHO'S WHO IN BASEBALL

Complete Life Records of More Than 200 Major League Ball Players

1930
FIFTEENTH EDITION

LEADING EVENTS PAST SEASON

BURLEIGH GRIMES
The Spit Ball King

Price 25c.

1930—BURLEIGH GRIMES

Born in Emerald, Wisconsin, Burleigh Grimes usually didn't shave on the day he pitched, perhaps to make himself look even more intimidating. This look earned him the nickname "Ol' Stubblebeard." When the spitball was outlawed in 1920, the 17 pitchers who made their living throwing it were allowed to finish their careers with the pitch. Two were later elected to the Hall of Fame—Stan Coveleski and Burleigh Grimes. Grimes was the last of the legal spitballers. His final game was on September 20, 1934.

In 1929 he won 17 games for the Pittsburgh Pirates, losing only seven. He struck out only 62. Grimes did not lead the league in any major statistic.

The Pirates finished the season in second place, 10½ games behind the champion Chicago Cubs.

Grimes had three stints with the Pirates, with whom he broke in in 1916, but over his 19-year major league career, he pitched for seven teams, ultimately winning 270 games.

Grimes was elected to the Baseball Hall of Fame in 1964.

In and Around Baseball 1929:

Rogers Hornsby of the Cubs was the National League's Most Valuable Player . . . The New York Yankees are the first team to put numbers on the back of their uniforms. Babe Ruth batted third, so he got #3. Lou Gehrig was the cleanup hitter, so he wore #4 . . . Wearing street clothes, Boston Braves owner Emil "Judge" Fuchs is the Braves' manager for 1929 . . . The Cleveland Indians Joe Sewell has 347 consecutive at-bats over 115 games without a strikeout. . . . August 11: Babe Ruth of the New York Yankees hits career home run #500.

The Philadelphia Athletics, managed by Connie Mack in street clothes, beat the Chicago Cubs 4–1 in the World Series.

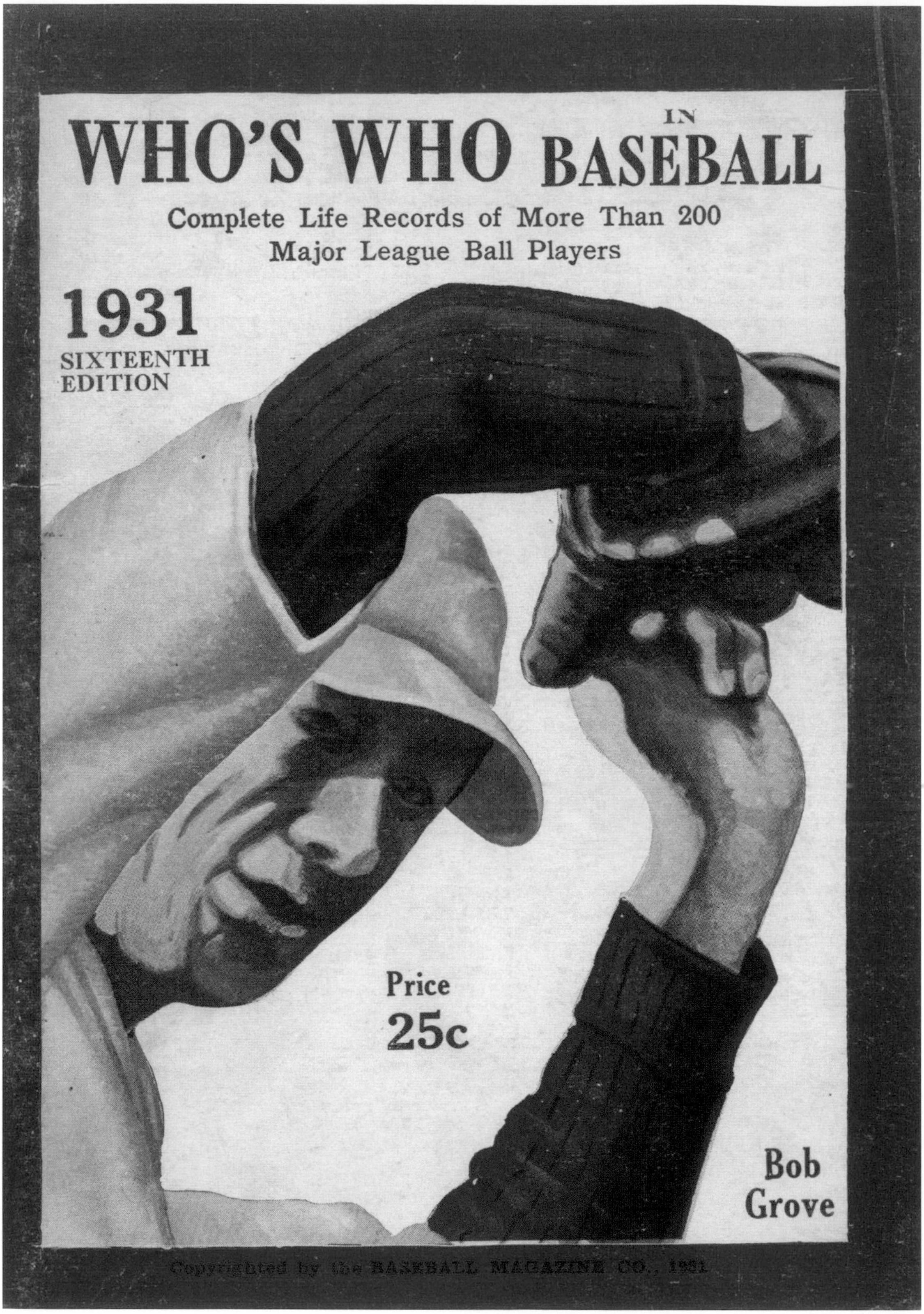
WHO'S WHO IN BASEBALL
Complete Life Records of More Than 200
Major League Ball Players
1931
SIXTEENTH
EDITION
Price
25c
Bob
Grove
Copyrighted by the BASEBALL MAGAZINE CO., 1931

1931—BOB GROVE

Robert Moses "Lefty" Grove (called "Bob Grove" on the cover of the 1931 edition of *Who's Who in Baseball*) spent his entire 19-year career in the American League, first with the Philadelphia Athletics and following an off-season 1933 trade, with the Boston Red Sox.

In 1930, Grove, from Lonaconing, Maryland, won the Triple Crown of Pitching, leading the AL with 28 wins, 209 strikeouts (one of seven consecutive years in which he led in Ks), and an ERA of 2.54. He won the pitching Triple Crown again in 1931—making him the second and the last man to accomplish that feat in consecutive seasons. (Grover Cleveland Alexander was the first in 1915–16.)

The A's won 102 games to take the pennant. Grove pitched for the A's in three consecutive World Series—1929 (won), 1930 (won), and 1931 (lost). He was 4-2 in eight Series games.

Grove was the best pitcher in the AL in nine seasons. He led the league in ERA for an unmatched eight seasons and in wins four times. Grove led the league in strikeouts for seven consecutive seasons (1925–1931), and had the best win-loss ratio for five seasons (1929, 1930, 1931, 1933, 1938). He was first in shutouts three times. Grove was the oldest player in the league in 1940 when he was 40 and again in 1941. He notched career win #300 on July 25, 1941—his final win. Grove was the 12th pitcher to win 300 games, the first since Grover Alexander in 1926, and the last until Warren Spahn in 1961. Grove holds the unenviable batting record for most career strikeouts by a pitcher: 593.

Grove was elected to the Hall of Fame in 1947.

In and Around Baseball 1930:

Bill Terry of the New York Giants bats .401, with 254 hits (still the National League record, tied with Lefty O'Doul) to set the record for most hits in a season, a mark which stood for 74 years as the major league standard, until broken by Ichiro Suzuki in 2004. . . Chuck Klein of the Philadelphia Phillies hits .386 and leads the NL with 158 runs scored and 59 doubles. He plays in all 156 games, and plays in every inning but one. He was ejected in the eighth inning on July 24 for arguing balls and strikes.

The Philadelphia Athletics won their last World Series, beating the St. Louis Cardinals 4–2.

WHO'S WHO IN BASEBALL

Complete Life Records of More Than 200 Major League Ball Players

SEVENTEENTH
EDITION

1932

Price
25c

Al
Simmons

1932—AL SIMMONS

Al Simmons (born Aloysius Szymanski), known as "Bucketfoot Al," led all of baseball with a .390 batting average in 1931 for the Philadelphia Athletics, who won the AL pennant. He won the batting title in 1930 too, with a .381 average.

At one time or another during his 20-year career with seven teams, Simmons led the league in hitting, runs scored, at-bats, RBIs, plate appearances, hits, and extra base hits. He hit over .380 three times. He was among the top five left fielders in assists and putouts eight times.

During his first twelve seasons, all with the A's, he led the majors with 1,827 hits and 343 doubles. His 90-year-old record for most hits in a season (253) by a right-handed batter, set in 1925, still stands. Simmons was voted into the Baseball Hall of Fame in 1953.

In and Around Baseball 1931:

April 29: Cleveland Indians pitcher Wes Ferrell bats .319 and hits nine home runs . . . During his no-hitter against the St. Louis Browns on April 29, he hits a two-run home run and retires his brother, Hall of Famer Rick, three times . . Earl Webb of the Boston Red Sox sets a single-season record that still stands 84 years later: 67 doubles . . . The 1931 New York Yankees are the only team ever to allow no passed balls. Bill Dickey caught 125 games. Arndt Jorgens, one of two Norwegian-born Yankees, caught in 40 games.

The 1931 World Series matched the same two teams as in 1930, but the outcome was different: the St. Louis Cardinals beat the Athletics 4–3.

WHO'S WHO IN BASEBALL
Price
25c
"Chuck"
Klein
Complete Life Records of more than 200 Major League Ball Players
EIGHTEENTH EDITION
1933
Copyrighted by the BASEBALL MAGAZINE CO., 1933

1933—CHUCK KLEIN

Chuck Klein had at least 200 hits in each of his first five full big-league seasons, 1929–1933. He hit a National League record 43 homers in 1929. In 1932 he played in all 154 games for the Philadelphia Phillies. Klein hit .348 and led the NL with 38 home runs (one of his four home run titles), 226 hits, 50 doubles, 15 triples, 152 runs scored, 420 total bases, and 20 stolen bases. Klein is the only modern player to lead the league in home runs and stolen bases in the same season. He was the NL Most Valuable Player, but the Phillies finished fourth in 1932, 23 games behind the NL champion Chicago Cubs.

Klein's numbers may have been helped because he played his home games in the Phillies' cozy Baker Bowl: During his years with the Phillies, Klein hit .420 at home, and .296 elsewhere. During the same period, he smacked 131 homers at home and 60 on the road.

In 1933, Klein won the NL Triple Crown, hitting .368 with 28 home runs and 120 RBIs.

In and Around Baseball 1932:

June 3: New York Yankees first baseman Lou Gehrig is the first modern player to hit four home runs in a game . . . Washington Senators pitcher Alvin "General" Crowder throws no wild pitches and doesn't hit a single batter in a league-leading 327 innings, during which he faced 1,356 batters.

October 1: World Series, Game 3: In the fifth inning at Wrigley Field, something happened that will be talked about as long as baseball is played: New York Yankee slugger Babe Ruth either did or did not "call his shot"—step out of the batter's box and point toward center field just before sending a home run right there. The Yankees swept the Chicago Cubs 4–0 to win the Series.

WHO'S WHO IN BASEBALL

Price
25c
NINETEENTH EDITION

Complete Life Records of More Than
220 Major League Ball Players

1934
Bill
Terry

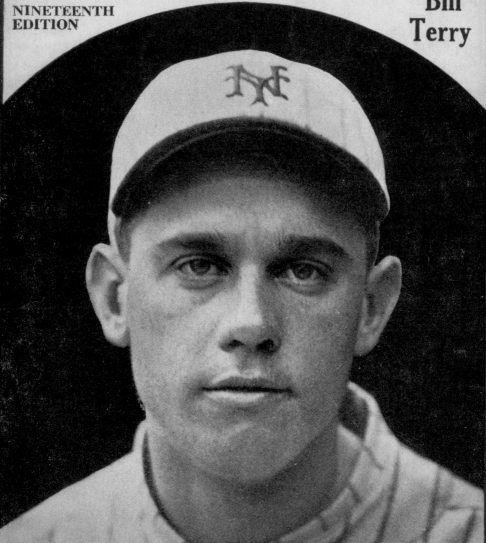

1934—BILL TERRY

Bill Terry was known as "Memphis Bill Terry," although he's from Atlanta. Terry spent his entire 14-year big-league career with the New York Giants, almost all of it at first base, where he excelled.

In 1930, he batted .401, with 254 hits (still the National League record, tied with Lefty O'Doul) to lead the league. His 254 hits stood as the major league record until broken by Ichiro Suzuki 74 years later, in 2004.

In 1933, Terry had a good year, but didn't lead the league in any major statistics. He hit .322, fourth best in the NL and was fifth in on-base percentage. Nevertheless, Terry was an All-Star.

Terry batted over .320 for nine consecutive seasons. He retired with a career .341 batting average—still the modern NL record for lefty batters. Terry later won three pennants managing the Giants.

He was elected to the Baseball Hall of Fame in 1954.

In and Around Baseball 1933:

July 6: 26 future Hall of Famers, including umpires and managers, participate in baseball's first All-Star Game, at Chicago's Comiskey Park. In the fifth inning, National League baseballs replaced American League balls. The American League won 4–2 . . . July 10: Chuck Klein of the Philadelphia Phillies hits four home runs in a 10-inning game . . . July 13: Babe Ruth hits home run #700.

For the only time in history, there were two Triple Crown winners, both in Philadelphia: Chuck Klein won the Triple Crown leading the NL with 28 home runs, 120 RBIs and a batting average of .368. In the AL, Jimmie Foxx of the Athletics won the Triple Crown with 48 home runs, 163 RBIs, and a .356 batting average.

The St. Louis Browns draw only 88,000 fans *all season*.

For the first time, three umpires becomes the norm.

As part of the renovations at Boston's Fenway Park, a new wall—later known as the "Green Monster"—is erected in left field.

The New York Giants returned to the World Series for the first time since 1924 and beat the Washington Senators 4–1.

WHO'S WHO IN BASEBALL

Complete Life
Records of more
than 220 Major
League Ball
Players

Price
25c

TWENTIETH
EDITION
1935

Dizzy
Dean

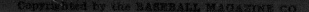

1935—DIZZY DEAN

Pitching for the St. Louis Cardinals in 1934, Jay Hannah "Dizzy" Dean, a native of Lucas, Arkansas, went 30-7, making him the last National Leaguer to win 30 games in one season. He led the league in wins, shutouts (7) and strikeouts (195). That was the third of four consecutive years in which he led in Ks.

Dean was named to the All-Star team, and was voted Most Valuable Player in the National League—just the second pitcher so honored.

Dean also pitched for the Cubs and Browns. Following his playing career, Dean became a broadcaster for the Cardinals, Browns, Yankees, The Mutual Network, ABC, and CBS—much to the chagrin of English teachers everywhere. (Example: "He slud into third base.")

In and Around Baseball 1934:
July 10: In the first inning of the second All-Star Game, Giants pitcher Carl Hubbell has a performance for the ages: He strikes out Babe Ruth, Lou Gehrig, and Jimmie Foxx in succession. In the second inning, he strikes out Al Simmons and Joe Cronin—five future Hall of Famers in a row . . . The New York Yankees boasted *two* Triple Crown winners: Lou Gehrig (49 home runs, 166 RBIs, and a batting average of .363), and pitcher Vernon "Lefty" Gomez, who wins the Triple Crown of Pitching with 26 wins, 158 strikeouts, and an ERA of 2.33. Even with powerhouse pitching and hitting, the Yankees finished in second place, seven games behind the AL champion Detroit Tigers and their MVP-winning catcher/manager Mickey Cochrane.

Dean pitches in three games of the 1934 World Series, including two complete game victories and one shutout. His brother Paul "Daffy" Dean won two in the Cardinals 4–3 Series victory over the Detroit Tigers. 🉑

1936—HANK GREENBERG

When he broke in with the Tigers for one game in 1930, "Hammerin'" Hank Greenberg was 19, the youngest player in the American League. A native New Yorker, Greenberg spent most of his career at first base.

On September 19, 1934, although his Tigers were locked in a pennant race, Greenberg decided to sit out the game in observance of Yom Kippur, the Jewish Day of Atonement.

In 1935, he led the American League with 36 home runs, 170 RBIs, 87 walks, and 389 total bases. Greenberg was the unanimous choice as AL Most Valuable Player. In 1937, Greenberg had 183 RBIs, just one shy of Lou Gehrig's AL record 184.

On May 7, 1941, Greenberg was inducted into the US Army. He was discharged as a sergeant on December 5, 1941—just two days before the attack on Pearl Harbor. On February 1, 1942, Greenberg re-enlisted. He became a first lieutenant in the Army Air Force, serving in India and Burma, and was discharged in 1945.

In 1947, following a salary dispute after 12 years in Detroit, Greenberg was sold to the Pittsburgh Pirates for $75,000. He became the first player to be paid $100,000 per year.

Greenberg—whose name is misspelled on the cover of *Who's Who in Baseball*—appeared in four World Series: 1934, 1935, 1940, and 1945 (he won that pennant with a 9th-inning grand slam in the last game of the season). He hit .318 with five World Series home runs. Greenberg was a four-time All-Star. He was the AL MVP in 1935 and 1940. He led the league in home runs four times (hitting a near-Ruthian 58 in 1938), extra base hits and RBIs four times, as well as total bases, doubles, and walks twice. He led in strikeouts only once. Greenberg was an excellent fielder, twice leading the American League in putouts and assists at first base.

Greenberg was present at the first Hall of Fame induction in 1939 and played in the first exhibition game at Cooperstown that year at the age of 28. He was elected to the Baseball Hall of Fame in 1956.

In and Around Baseball 1935:

May 24: President Franklin Roosevelt throws a switch at the White House to turn on the lights at Cincinnati's Crosley Field for baseball's first night game.

Greenberg led the Tigers to a 4–2 victory over the Chicago Cubs (winners of 100 games in the regular season) in the World Series.

WHO'S WHO IN BASEBALL

Price
25c

TWENTY-
SECOND
EDITION

Complete Life Records of More Than
220 Major League Ball Players

LOU
GEHRIG
1937

1937—LOU GEHRIG

Lou Gehrig's nickname, when he was a kid, was "Babe." Later, he was known as "The Iron Horse." He attended Columbia University in his native New York City, and spent three years in the minors before becoming a Yankee in 1923.

Gehrig won the American League Most Valuable player Award in 1927. In 1930, Gehrig drove in 173 runs, including 117 *just in road games*. After 84 years, his 185 RBIs in 1931 is still the American League record.

In 1934, Gehrig won the Triple Crown—the only man to do so in his hometown—hitting .363 with 49 home runs (his third home run title) and 166 RBIs. He also made himself into an excellent first baseman. But the AL Most Valuable Player Award went to Mickey Cochrane, because of a rule (later abandoned) prohibiting repeat winners.

In 1936, the first year after Babe Ruth, his teammate for 11 years (1923–1934) retired, Gehrig led the league with 49 home runs, 167 runs scored, and 130 walks while batting .354, fifth behind Luke Appling's .388. The Yankees won 102 games and the AL pennant and went on to beat their crosstown rivals the New York Giants 4–2 in the World Series, their first of four titles in a row, and the fifth of Gehrig's seven World Series. His Yankees won six of them.

Gehrig was an All-Star again in 1936—his fifth of seven All-Star elections—and won his second AL MVP. His .478 on-base percentage and .696 slugging percentage led the league, as did his 342 times on base. He was second in RBIs and total bases.

Gehrig scored over 100 runs and drove in over 100 runs for 13 consecutive years. He had a career batting average of .340. His record of 23 career grand slams stood for 75 years until broken by another Yankee, Alex Rodriguez, in 2013.

For 14 years, between June 1, 1925, and May 2, 1939, Gehrig played in 2,130 consecutive games, setting a titanic record that stood for 56 years until broken on September 6, 1995, by Cal Ripken Jr. of the Baltimore Orioles. Ironically, Wally Pipp, the first baseman replaced by Gehrig in 1925, was at the 1939 game in Detroit when Gehrig benched himself.

July 4, 1939, was Lou Gehrig Appreciation Day at Yankee Stadium. 62,0000 fans heard his famous speech, containing the immortal line, "Today, I consider myself the luckiest man on the face of the Earth." His #4 became the first uniform number retired—a true symbol of respect. He remains the only Yankee ever to wear #4.

In 1939, following his retirement because of amyotrophic lateral sclerosis (ALS), which would later become known as Lou Gehrig's Disease, he was inducted into the Baseball Hall of Fame by a special election—the only man elected in a year in which he played. One of the greatest players in history, Gehrig died in 1941 at the age of 37.

In and Around Baseball 1936:

July 10: Chuck Klein of the Philadelphia Phillies becomes the second man and the first National Leaguer to hit four home runs in a game . . . Babe Ruth, Ty Cobb, Honus Wagner, Walter Johnson, and Christy Mathewson are the first five players named to the as-yet-unbuilt Baseball Hall of Fame . . . A new era in baseball travel is inaugurated as the Boston Red Sox fly from Chicago to St. Louis.

The 1936 World Series was the first Subway Series since 1923 as the New York Yankees beat the New York Giants 4–2.

1938—JOE MEDWICK

Joe Medwick was called "Ducky Wucky" because of the way he walked. But there was nothing funny about the way he played. In 1937, as a member of the St. Louis Cardinals' "Gas House Gang," Medwick won the Triple Crown—the last National Leaguer to do so—and was the National League Most Valuable Player. He led all players with a .374 batting average, 237 hits, and 56 doubles and was tops in the NL with 31 home runs, 156 games played, 633 at-bats, 111 runs scored, 154 RBIs, and 406 total bases. But his St. Louis Cardinals finished third, 15 games behind the NL champion New York Giants.

Between 1935 and 1938, he led the NL in just about everything: batting average, slugging percentage, on-base percentage, games played, at-bats, runs scored, and home runs once; hits and doubles twice; total bases, extra base hits, and RBIs three times; and putouts in left field four times. Medwick was a 10-time All-Star.

Medwick, who played most of his career in left field, appeared in the World Series in 1934 with the Cardinals and 1941 with the St. Louis Browns. He hit over .300 15 times, retiring with a career batting average of .324.

In an infamous incident, baseball commissioner Kenesaw Mountain Landis ordered Medwick removed in the bottom of the 6th inning of Game 7 of the 1934 World Series for his own safety, as he was being pummeled with debris by the fans at Detroit's Navin Field, irate over an earlier play.

Medwick was elected to the Baseball Hall of Fame in 1968.

In and Around Baseball 1937:

April 19: Bob Feller was just 18 when he became the youngest baseball player ever to appear on the cover of *Time* magazine . . . April 20: Gee Walker of the Detroit Tigers becomes the only man ever to hit for the cycle on Opening Day . . . July 7: Dizzy Dean is hit in the toe by an Earl Averill line drive during the All-Star Game. He came back before fully recovering with an altered pitching motion that shortened his career . . . August 20: Mel Ott becomes the first National Leaguer to hit 300 career home runs . . . The New York Yankees' Lefty Gomez won his second Triple Crown of Pitching: 21 wins, 194 strikeouts, and a 2.33 ERA. But no MVP.

It was an ALL–New York World Series as the Yankees, winners of 102 regular season games, faced the New York Giants. The Yankees won 4–1.

WHO'S WHO IN BASEBALL

1939
TWENTY-
FOURTH
EDITION

PRICE
25c

JAMES EMORY FOXX

1939—JIMMIE FOXX

Jimmie Foxx, known as "The Beast" and "Double X," was only 17 when he was discovered by Frank "Home Run" Baker. Foxx joined the Philadelphia Athletics in 1925, when he was the youngest player in the league, and played in the major leagues for 20 years with the A's, Boston Red Sox, Chicago Cubs, and Philadelphia Phillies.

In 1933, Foxx won the American League Triple Crown with 48 home runs, 163 RBIs, and a batting average of .356.

In 1938, he hit 50 home runs, a feat previously accomplished only by Babe Ruth (four times) and Hack Wilson. Foxx would have won the home run crown, but Hank Greenberg hit 58 homers that season. Foxx hit .349 while driving in 175 runs to lead both leagues. He also led both leagues (for the third time) with 398 total bases. Foxx led the AL with a .462 on-base percentage, a .704 slugging percentage, 398 total bases, 98 extra base hits, 316 times on base, and 119 walks (tied with Greenberg). On June 16, he became the first American Leaguer to walk six times in a nine-inning game. But his Athletics finished dead last in the American League, 46 games behind the pennant-winning New York Yankees.

In 1938, he was selected for the AL All-Star team (one of nine All-Star selections), and was named the league's Most Valuable Player as he had been in 1932 and 1933.

Foxx hit the most home runs in the 1930s—415, and was the second man after Babe Ruth to hit 500 homers. Although his achievements have been eclipsed, Foxx was the youngest player to hit 100 home runs (23), 200 (25), 300 (27), 400 (30), and 500 (32).

Foxx played mostly first and third base, occasionally catching. But in 1945, he won a game pitching for the Phillies.

Foxx was inducted into the Baseball Hall of Fame in 1951. His wife died after choking to death on food. Foxx also died after choking to death on a piece of steak.

In and Around Baseball 1938:

In his first full season in the majors, Cincinnati Reds left-hander Johnny Vander Meer—"The Dutch Master"—pitches consecutive no-hitters on June 11 and June 15—a feat unmatched in baseball history . . . August 2: As an experiment, yellow baseballs are used in a Dodgers-Cardinals game at Ebbets Field.

The New York Yankees sweep the Chicago Cubs in the 1938 World Series.

WHO'S WHO in BASEBALL

PRICE
25c

1940
TWENTY-
FIFTH
EDITION

"BUCKY"
WALTERS

1940—BUCKY WALTERS

William "Bucky" Walters pitched for 16 years for Philadelphia Phillies, Cincinnati Reds, and Boston Braves. He was with the Phillies in 1936 when he led all National League pitchers with 21 losses.

In 1939, as a Red, he won the National League Triple Crown of Pitching with 27 wins (he also led in 1940 and 1944) and an ERA of 2.29 (he led in 1940 too) in 319 innings pitched with 137 strikeouts. A fastball pitcher who threw sidearm, Walters was a workhorse in 1939, pitching 31 complete games, and facing a league-leading 1,283 batters. He earned an All-Star berth and was the second of three Red players in a row to be the NL's MVP: 1938—Ernie Lombardi, 1939—Walters, 1940—Frank McCormick. Walters' salary was reported to be $22,000.

Walters was a six-time All-Star and was the league leader in innings pitched and complete games three consecutive years, 1939–1941. He was also an excellent fielder, once leading the NL in putouts and another time in assists. His World Series record was 2-2. Walters frequently helped his cause with his bat: he had a career batting average of .243.

Walters played for the Phillies against the Reds in the first night game on May 24, 1935, and, on August 26, 1939, for the Reds in the first televised ballgame.

Following his playing career, he was a scout, coach, umpire, and manager of the Reds. Walters was the first player to appear on the cover of *Who's Who in Baseball* who did not become a Hall of Famer.

In and Around Baseball 1939:

May 16: The Philadelphia Athletics host the Cleveland Indians in the first American League night game . . . June 12: The National Baseball Hall of Fame and Museum opens in Cooperstown, New York. Those inducted were 12 of the game's immortals: Ty Cobb, Babe Ruth, Walter Johnson, Grover Cleveland Alexander, Honus Wagner, Cy Young, Eddie Collins, Tris Speaker, Nap Lajoie, Connie Mack, Christy Mathewson, and George Sisler . . . Starting in 1939, the All-Star Game had to include at least one player from each major league team.

The Reds are swept by the New York Yankees in the World Series.

WHO'S WHO in BASEBALL

1941
TWENTY-SIXTH
EDITION

BOB
FELLER

PRICE
25¢

1941—BOB FELLER

"Rapid" Robert Feller burst into the majors with the Cleveland Indians in 1936 as a fireballing 17-year-old from Van Meter, Iowa. He was the youngest player in the American League in 1936 and again in 1937. On August 23, 1936, his first start, the 17-year-old struck out 15 St. Louis Browns. On September 13, 1936, he struck out his age: 17 strikeouts—a new American League record—against the Philadelphia Athletics. At the end of the season, Feller returned to Van Meter to finish high school.

In 1939, Feller was the first pitcher to win 24 games before turning 21. But his Indians finished the season twenty and one-half games behind the AL champion New York Yankees.

His 1940 season was memorable: Feller won the Triple Crown of Pitching in the American League (but not the MVP—that went to Hank Greenberg) with 27 victories, 261 strikeouts, and an ERA of 2.61. He also led the AL with 37 starts, 31 complete games, four shutouts, and 1,304 batters faced.

Feller enlisted in the Navy on December 8, 1941, the day after the bombing of Pearl Harbor. He won six campaign ribbons and eight Battle Stars as a chief petty officer of a gun crew on the battleship *Alabama*. He fought in the battles for Kwajalein, the Gilbert and Marshall Islands, and Truk. In later years, when the winner of 266 games was asked which of his victories was the most memorable, he always gave the same answer: "World War II!"

He lost nearly four prime years—1942, 1943, 1944, and part of 1945—of his pitching career to the Navy, but was never bitter about the pitching records he might have set. But he did have his original Hall of Fame plaque changed from "1936–1956" to "1936–1941, 1945–1956" to reflect his years of Navy service.

Feller set the modern record for most strikeouts in a game with 18 on October 2, 1938, a record that stood for 31 years. In 1946, Feller set the record (since broken) for most strikeouts in a season with 348.

In 1948, Feller pitched in his only World Series. He lost both games he pitched, but the Indians beat the Boston Braves 4–2.

In 2013, the Bob Feller Act of Valor Award was created to honor a Hall of Famer, an active major leaguer, and a chief petty officer in the US Navy.

Feller pitched three no-hitters and led the American League in wins six times, winning at least 20 games six times. He led the league in strikeouts seven times; innings pitched five times; complete games three times; and shutouts four. Feller, an eight-time All-Star, was elected to the Baseball Hall of Fame in 1962.

In and Around Baseball 1940:

April 16: 21-year-old Bob Feller of the Indians does something which no major leaguer has done before or since: He throws a no-hitter on Opening Day to beat the White Sox in Chicago . . . September 24: Jimmie Foxx of the Boston Red Sox becomes just the second player to hit his 500th career home run.

The Cincinnati Reds beat the Detroit Tigers 4–3 in the 1940 World Series.

WHO'S WHO in BASEBALL

1942
TWENTY-SEVENTH
EDITION

JOE
DI MAGGIO

PRICE
25¢

1942—JOE DIMAGGIO

"Joltin'" Joe DiMaggio, "The Yankee Clipper," broke in with the New York Yankees in 1936, when he hit .323 and led the major leagues with 15 triples. He's the only player to win world championships in his first four years in the majors: 1936, 1937, 1938, and 1939.

DiMaggio, a native of Martinez, California, hit 30 home runs in 1941 and drove in 125 runs to lead the majors. He also led with 348 total bases. DiMaggio was an All-Star—as he was during *every* year of his 13-year career—and led the Yankees to a world championship, beating the Brooklyn Dodgers 4–1.

But DiMaggio accomplished something in 1941 that has never been approached in major league baseball: Between May 15 and July 16, he hit safely in 56 consecutive games, batting .408 during the streak. He beat out Boston's Ted Williams (who hit .406, the last player to bat over .400) for the American League's Most Valuable Player Award, one of his three MVPs.

DiMaggio won the AL batting title twice, and played in 51 World Series games, but perhaps the most telling statistic about DiMaggio's fabled career is this: 361 career home runs, only 369 career strikeouts. If not for what he considered his subpar 1951 season, his last, in which at age 36 he hit only .263, he would have retired with more home runs (349) than strikeouts (333).

DiMaggio missed the 1943, 1944, and 1945 seasons to serve in the US Army Air Force as a staff sergeant. His salary went from a reported $43,750 per year to $50 per month.

His uniform #5 was retired by the Yankees in 1952, the year after his retirement. DiMaggio, the consummate, graceful professional, was elected to the Baseball Hall of Fame in 1955.

In and Around Baseball 1941:

June 1: The New York Giants' Mel Ott hits career home run #400, the first National Leaguer to reach that mark . . . July 8: Boston Red Sox slugger Ted Williams comes to bat in the bottom of the ninth inning in the All-Star Game in Detroit. With the AL losing 5–4, Williams hits a three-run walk-off home run off the fencing of the roof at Briggs Stadium, one of the most dramatic ever in the Mid-Summer Classic . . . September 28, the last day of the season: Ted Williams's batting average is .399955. If he sits out the final games, it will be rounded off to .400—making him the first American Leaguer to hit .400 since Harry Heilmann hit .403 in 1923. But Williams plays in both games of a doubleheader against the Philadelphia Athletics. He goes 6 for 8 and finishes with a batting average of .406, the highest in the majors in 67 years . . . The Brooklyn Dodgers are the first team to use batting helmets.

The 1941 World Series is another all–New York City affair, pitting the New York Yankees against the Brooklyn Dodgers, making their first appearance in the Fall Classic since they lost in 1920. The Yankees win 4–1.

WHO'S WHO in BASEBALL

1943
TWENTY-EIGHTH
EDITION

TED
WILLIAMS

PRICE
25¢

1943—TED WILLIAMS

Ted Williams said that his ambition in life was that when he walked down the street, people would say "There goes the greatest hitter that ever lived." Many believe he achieved his dream.

In 1939, Williams was the first rookie to lead the American League in RBIs (145). "The Splendid Splinter" was a star from his rookie season, when he hit 31 home runs, batted .327, and led the AL with 344 total bases. He played his entire 19-year career for the Boston Red Sox, interrupted by five years as a Marine pilot in World War II and in Korea, where he flew 39 combat missions.

In 1942, his last year before joining the US Marines, Williams won his first of two Triple Crowns, leading the American League with 36 homers, batting .356—one of his six batting crowns—and 137 RBIs. He led the league in on-base percentage (one of 12 times he led in that stat), extra base hits (75), and slugging. He also walked 145 times, one of eight times he was tops in the AL in walks, probably the reason he did not have 3,000 hits. He was an All-Star (one of 17 selections), but lost the MVP award to Joe Gordon of the American League champion New York Yankees. Gordon, a future Hall of Famer, hit 18 homers, batted .322, and drove in 103 runs and led the AL in errors, grounding into double plays, and strikeouts. Williams won the Triple Crown again in 1947—32 homers, 114 RBIs, .343 batting average—becoming the only player besides Rogers Hornsby to win it twice. Williams didn't win the AL MVP award in 1947, either. Joe DiMaggio did.

Williams was respected, of course, but was not particularly well liked by the fans or the sportswriters in Boston, where he never bought a home. The San Diego native lived at the team hotel.

Williams hit 521 career home runs and retired with 2,654 hits. Who knows what his numbers might have been but for the five years he lost in the Marines?

At his Hall of Fame induction speech in 1966, Williams—tieless, as usual—made a heartfelt plea for induction of the great Negro League stars.

In and Around Baseball 1942:

January 14: Just over a month after Pearl Harbor, commissioner Kenesaw Mountain Landis wrote to President Franklin Roosevelt, offering to put baseball at the government's disposal: If the president wanted baseball halted for the duration of the war, Landis was prepared to do that.

But FDR wrote to Landis on January 15, 1942, in what became known as "The Green Light Letter": "I honestly feel that it would be best for the country to keep baseball going. There will be fewer people unemployed and everybody will work longer hours and harder than ever before. And that means that they ought to have a chance for recreation and for taking their minds off their work even more than before. Baseball provides a recreation which does not last over two hours or two hours and a half, and which can be got for very little cost. [Times have changed!] And, incidentally, I hope that night games can be extended because it gives an opportunity to the day shift to see a game occasionally." . . . May 13: Boston Braves pitcher Jim Tobin hits three home runs to beat the Chicago Cubs 6–5—the only modern pitcher to hit three homers in one game. Except for the cancellation of the 1945 All-Star Game because of travel restrictions, baseball kept going during World War II. Proceeds from the sale of tickets to the 1942 All-Star Game at Brooklyn's Ebbets Field were to go to the war effort. So, although the Dodgers were the official "hosts," the game was moved to the Giants' home, the Polo Grounds, which seated more fans. The AL won 3–1 . . . August 23: 69,000 fans are on hand at Yankee Stadium when, between games of a doubleheader, 55-year-old Walter Johnson throws 19 pitches to 47-year-old Babe Ruth. Ruth hits one into the stands. The event raises $80,000 for the Army-Navy Relief Fund . . . Danny Litwhiler played every game of the season in the outfield for the Philadelphia Phillies and made no errors.

The 1942 World Series matched the St. Louis Cardinals, winners of 106 games during the regular season with the New York Yankees, who won 103. The Cardinals won this first wartime Series 4–1.

WHO'S WHO in BASEBALL

1944
TWENTY-NINTH
EDITION

STAN
MUSIAL

PRICE
25¢

1944—STAN MUSIAL

Stan "The Man" Musial, from Donora, Pennsylvania (also the birthplace of Ken Griffey Sr. and Jr.), came up to the majors in 1941. He hit .426 in 12 games with the St. Louis Cardinals, for whom he played his entire 22-year career—a Cardinal record. In 1942, he hit .315, but Musial came into his own in 1943, when he won his first of three National League Most Valuable Player Awards batting .357 with 220 hits in 700 plate appearances—all league-leading figures. Musial was also MVP in 1946 and 1948. Musial hit just 13 home runs, but led the majors with 48 doubles and 20 triples. He also led in slugging percentage and on-base percentage. The Cardinals won 105 games and the NL pennant.

Musial led the NL in hitting seven times, and had the most total bases and the most hits six times. He led in doubles eight times, and triples five. He hit over .300 18 times and retired (after 3,026 games, a record at the time) with a .331 career average and 475 home runs—the most ever by someone who never won a single-season home run title. His best was 39 homers in 1948. He had 3,630 hits—fourth all time, and most in the National League when he retired after the 1963 season: 1,815 at home, 1,815 on the road. Musial played 929 games in left field and 1,016 at first base.

Musial was selected for a record 24 All-Star Games—tied with Willie Mays and Hank Aaron—and still holds the records for most career All-Star Game home runs (6), most pinch-hit at-bats (10), and most games played as a pinch-hitter (10).

In and Around Baseball 1943:

The Chicago White Sox play a record 44 doubleheaders.

It's the Cardinals versus the Yankees again in the World Series. This time, the Yankees win 4–1.

WHO'S WHO in BASEBALL

1945
THIRTIETH
EDITION

HAL NEWHOUSER
AND
PAUL TROUT

PRICE
25¢

1945—HAL NEWHOUSER, PAUL TROUT

The cover of the 1945 edition of *Who's Who in Baseball* was the first to feature two players, both pitchers for the Detroit Tigers in 1944.

In 1944, 23-year-old Hal Newhouser was the Most Valuable Player in the American League and was voted *The Sporting News* Major League Player of the Year. The Tigers finished the season one game behind the unlikely champions, the St. Louis Browns.

He broke into the majors in 1939 when he was just 18—the youngest player in the league that year and the next—and spent 15 years with the Tigers, followed by two with the Cleveland Indians.

Newhouser was an All-Star in six seasons. He was elected to the Baseball Hall of Fame in 1992.

In 1944, Paul "Dizzy" Trout, a native of Sandcut, Indiana, led the American League with 40 games started, 33 complete games, 352.1 innings pitched, and 1,421 batters faced. He also led the AL with an ERA of 2.12 and pitched a majors-leading seven shutouts. His won-loss record was 27 wins (second to Newhouser's 29) with 14 losses.

Trout pitched for the Tigers for 14 seasons, then spent one with the Boston Red Sox and one with the Baltimore Orioles. He pitched in the World Series in 1940 and 1945, going 1-2. Trout was an All-Star in 1944 and 1947. His son Steve "Rainbow" Trout pitched in the majors for 12 years.

In and Around Baseball 1944:

No major league games are played on D-Day, June 6 . . . June 10: 15-year-old Joe Nuxhall pitches for the Cincinnati Reds—the youngest major leaguer ever.

In 1944 the St. Louis Browns win the American League pennant for the first and last time. They face their intra-city rivals the St. Louis Cardinals in the "Trolley Series." Both teams share Sportsman's Park, so all seven games are played at the same stadium—the first time that had happened since 1922, when the Giants and the Yankees played at the Polo Grounds. This is also the last time that all World Series games are played in one park. The Cardinals win 4–2.

In a unique aspect to the all–St. Louis World Series, Cardinals manager Billy Southworth—a future Hall of Famer—and Browns manager Luke Sewell share a one-bedroom apartment in St. Louis. During the regular season, it was rare for both to be home at the same time.

WHO'S WHO in BASEBALL

1946
THIRTY-FIRST
EDITION

HAL NEWHOUSER

PRICE
25¢

1946—HAL NEWHOUSER

In 1946, Hal Newhouser became the first player since Babe Ruth in 1920 and 1921 to appear on the cover of *Who's Who in Baseball* in consecutive years.

Some thought that Newhouser's 1944 success was because many big leaguers, including some of the game's big stars, were in military service during World War II. Newhouser had planned to enlist in the US Army Air Force in July 1942 and be inducted on the pitcher's mound at Detroit's Briggs Stadium. But during his Army physical, doctors detected mitral valve prolapse, a heart condition. Newhouser was 4-F. "Prince Hal" was unsuccessful in later attempts to get around the Army's rejection.

In 1945, Newhouser led the majors with 25 wins, an ERA of 1.81, and 212 strikeouts to win the pitching Triple Crown. He pitched 29 complete games, 313.1 innings, and eight shutouts—all tops in the American League.

When the stars returned to baseball from military service in 1946, Newhouser *again* led the league in wins (26) and ERA (1.94). He was second in strikeouts that year, with 275. (Bob Feller, back from service in the US Navy, picked up where he left off. He led the AL with 348 strikeouts.) Newhouser won the MVP again in 1945, becoming the only pitcher to ever win back-to-back MVP Awards.

In and Around Baseball 1945:

Although All-Star teams were chosen for both leagues, no All-Star Game was held because of World War II travel restrictions . . . One-armed Pete Gray (born Wyshner) played the outfield for the St. Louis Browns in 1945, his only year in the majors. He hit .218 with six doubles, two triples, and five stolen bases . . . April 24: US senator (and former Kentucky governor) Albert B. "Happy" Chandler is unanimously elected the second commissioner of baseball . . . August 1: Mel Ott of the New York Giants becomes the third player (after Babe Ruth and Jimmie Foxx) to hit 500 career home runs . . . August 19: Foxx, a member of the 500 home run club, pitches seven innings for the Philadelphia Phillies and earns the only win of his career . . . New York Yankees second baseman George "Snuffy" Stirnweiss had not led the American League in batting all season. But by going 3 for 5 on September 30, in a 12–2 drubbing of the Boston Red Sox, Stirnweiss raises his batting average to .3085443—the highest in the American League. And because September 30 is the last day of the season, he's the AL batting champion. His average was .000866 higher than Tony Cuccinello's . . . The Washington Senators hit just one home run at home all season—an inside-the-parker by Joe Kuhel.

In the World Series, Clyde McCullough of the Chicago Cubs did an extremely rare thing: He came up to bat in Game 7 although, because of military service, he had not played at all during the regular season. He struck out. The Tigers beat the Cubs 4–3 in the Series. The Cubs have not been to the World Series since, a drought of 70 years.

WHO'S WHO in BASEBALL

1947
THIRTY-SECOND
EDITION

EDDIE DYER
(Manager of the St. Louis Cardinals)

PRICE
25c

1947—EDDIE DYER

Eddie Dyer went to Rice on an athletic scholarship. He had a short career as a starter and reliever for the St. Louis Cardinals from 1922 to 1927. His career record was 15-15, with an ERA of 4.76.

But Dyer, a native of Morgan City, Louisiana, made the cover of *Who's Who in Baseball* as the manager of the 1946 Cardinals, the only manager who was not a player/manager so honored. He succeeded Hall of Famer Billy Southworth, who was the manager in 1929 and again from 1940 to 1945. Dyer was the Cardinals skipper from 1946 to 1950.

In 1946, Dyer managed the St. Louis Cardinals to a 4–3 World Series victory over the Boston Red Sox. His 1946 team featured Howie Pollet, Marty Marion, Whitey Kurowski, Harry Breechen, Harry "The Hat" Walker, Terry Moore, Joe Garagiola, and Hall of Famers Stan Musial, Red Schoendienst, and Enos Slaughter.

The highlight of the Series was a play in the bottom of the eighth inning of Game 7 at St. Louis's Sportsman's Park with the score tied at 3. It is still considered one of the most memorable moments in baseball history.

Enos Slaughter singled to center. Kurowski bunted to the pitcher and was out. Del Rice flied out to left field. Harry "The Hat" Walker hit the ball to center field, where Leon Culberson had replaced the injured Dom DiMaggio. Slaughter was off with the pitch. Culberson fielded the ball and threw to Red Sox shortstop Johnny Pesky—a 1946 All-Star—who checked Walker at first base. But Slaughter didn't stop at third. By the time Pesky's throw got to Red Sox catcher Roy Partee, it was too late. "Slaughter's Mad Dash" had allowed him to score what turned out to be the winning run. The Red Sox didn't score in the top of the ninth and the Cardinals won the game 4–3. For years, Johnny Pesky was unfairly blamed for holding, or somehow delaying his throw home.

In and Around Baseball 1946:

June 9: Ted Williams hits the longest home run ever hit at Boston's Fenway Park—into the lower bleachers, specifically into the head of a fan seated 502 feet from home plate in section 42, row 37, seat 21. To mark the spot, the seat was painted red in 1984 . . . July 9: In the eighth inning of the first postwar All-Star Game, pitcher Rip Sewell of the National League Pittsburgh Pirates throws his unique Eephus pitch—a very slow arc ball—to Ted Williams of the American League Boston Red Sox, who fouls it off. Williams parks the next pitch—also a Eephus ball—in the bullpen. AL 12, NL 0 . . . Bob Feller of the Cleveland Indians strikes out 348, a new 20th-century record.

The World Series pitted the NL's St. Louis Cardinals against the Boston Red Sox, making their first Fall Classic appearance since they won in 1918. The Cardinals won 4–3.

WHO'S WHO in BASEBALL

1948
THIRTY-THIRD
EDITION

RALPH KINER and JOHN MIZE
(Home Run Twins of 1947)

PRICE
30c

1948—RALPH KINER, JOHNNY MIZE

The cover photo of 1948's *Who's Who in Baseball* features Ralph Kiner and Johnny Mize in a single picture.

Ralph Kiner was born in Santa Rita, one of only 27 major leaguers from New Mexico. He served as a Navy pilot during World War II.

In 1947 Kiner batted .313 and hit 51 home runs for the Pittsburgh Pirates to tie with Johnny Mize for the National League home run crown. Kiner was the first Pirate to win the NL home run crown since Tommy Leach led the league in 1902 with six. The Pirates gave Kiner an $8,000 bonus.

In 1947 Kiner also led the majors with a .639 slugging percentage and 361 total bases. On August 16, he became the first Pirate to hit three home runs in a game. He scored 118 runs and drove in 127. Kiner led the league in putouts by a left fielder with 384. But Pittsburgh finished tied for last in the National League, 32 games behind the NL champion Brooklyn Dodgers, making Kiner the only player to hit at least 50 homers for a last-place team.

In 1949, he hit 54, just two below Hack Wilson's NL record 56. Kiner is the first National Leaguer to hit at least 50 home runs in a single season twice. Kiner spent eight years with the Pirates, two with the Chicago Cubs, and one with the Cleveland Indians. He retired with 369 career home runs and won or tied for the lead in home runs during his first seven years in the National League—a feat unmatched in baseball history. Kiner was a six-time All-Star.

After his playing days, Kiner broadcast White Sox games for one year, then spent 50 years broadcasting New York Mets games. He was elected to the Baseball Hall of Fame in 1975.

Standing 6'2" and weighing 215 pounds, Johnny Mize was known as "The Big Cat." Mize spent the first six years of his career with the St. Louis Cardinals. He won the National League batting crown in 1939, hitting .349. Mize led the NL in total bases from 1938 to 1940.

After serving in the US Navy from 1943 to 1945, he returned to the majors to play five years with the New York Giants, then five seasons with the New York Yankees.

In 1947, as a Giant, Mize led the NL in home runs for the third time with 51, his single-season best. Mize's hit #50 just two days after Kiner hit his 50th. They finished the season tied at 51. Mize is the only man to hit at least 50 homers but strike out fewer than 50 times (42). Mize tied Kiner again in 1948 with 40 homers. He had 138 RBIs to lead the NL for the third time, and a league-leading 137 runs scored. His 79 extra base hits were also tops in the NL, the fourth time he had led in that category.

Mize was no slouch as a first baseman: In 1947 he led the league with 1,381 putouts and a fielding percentage of .996.

Mize was on five consecutive world championship teams with the Yankees, 1949–1953, hitting a combined .264. He hit three home runs in a game six times. His regular season career batting average was .312. Mize retired with four home run titles and 359 career homers.

Mize was elected to the Baseball Hall of Fame in 1981.

In and Around Baseball 1947:

The players' pension fund is established . . . April 15: A revolutionary upheaval in the game: Jack Roosevelt Robinson, who had been a lieutenant in the US Army and a four-letter man at UCLA, made his debut with the Brooklyn Dodgers—the first black man to play in the modern major leagues. He was the first Rookie of the Year (one award for both leagues), and led the Dodgers to the National League pennant. In 1962, he was elected to the Hall of Fame . . . July 5: Larry Doby, the first black man to play in the American League, made his debut with the Cleveland Indians. He too was elected to the Baseball Hall of Fame . . . September 22: Robinson appears on the cover of *Time* magazine.

The 1947 World Series, the first to be televised, matched the Brooklyn Dodgers with the New York Yankees. In Game 4 on October 3, Yankee pitcher Bill Bevens pitches a no-hitter into the ninth inning. Dodgers pinch hitter Harry "Cookie" Lavagetto doubles with two outs. Dodgers win the game 3–2, but lose the "Subway Series" 4–3.

WHO'S WHO in BASEBALL

1949
THIRTY-FOURTH
EDITION

LOU BOUDREAU

PRICE
30c
(35c in Canada)

1949—LOU BOUDREAU

Lou Boudreau, a native of Harvey, Illinois, came to the Cleveland Indians from the University of Illinois—where he was the captain of both the basketball and baseball teams—as a 20-year-old in 1938. Four years later, as a 24-year-old, he started his nine-year career as the team's player-manager. Boudreau won the American League batting title in 1944.

Boudreau, considered the best shortstop of the 1940s, was the AL batting champion as a player-manager in 1944. In 1948, Boudreau was elected to the All-Star team as a shortstop—one of seven selections. On the final day of the season in a classic game against the Boston Red Sox, Boudreau went 4 for 4 with two home runs to lead his team to an 8–3 victory and the AL championship.

Boudreau was also *The Sporting News* Major League Player of the Year in 1948. He hit .355 (second in the American League behind Ted Williams's .369), was second in times on base, third in hits and RBIs, fourth in singles and total bases, fifth in runs scored, sixth in extra base hits and walks, and seventh in doubles.

Boudreau is the only man to appear on the cover of *Who's Who in Baseball* whose son-in-law also appeared on the cover. Denny McLain, on the cover in 1969, was married to Boudreau's daughter Sharon.

Boudreau also played briefly for the Boston Red Sox and managed the Red Sox, Kansas City Athletics, and Chicago Cubs.

He was elected to the Baseball Hall of Fame in 1970. A street adjacent to Municipal Stadium in Cleveland was named in his honor, and the Indians retired his uniform #5.

Boudreau devised a strategy—relatively new at the time—to defend against Ted Williams's tendency to pull the ball: Boudreau shifted the Indians' shortstop to play on the right side of the infield.

Boudreau went on to a 30-year career broadcasting games for the Chicago Cubs.

In and Around Baseball 1948:

Briggs (later Tiger) Stadium, home of the Detroit Tigers, is the last American League stadium to add lights for night games . . . June 30: Bob Lemon of the Indians pitches the first American League no-hitter at night, beating the Tigers 2–0 in Detroit . . . July 9: After many years as a star in the Negro Leagues, Satchel Paige, approximately 42 years old, makes his major league debut with the Indians. He's the oldest rookie ever . . . July 18: Pat Seerey of the Chicago White Sox hits four home runs in a game against the Philadelphia Athletics . . . Ted Williams comes within a whisker of winning an unprecedented third Triple Crown, leading the American League with 39 home runs and 159 RBIs, but George Kell of the Detroit Tigers ends the year with a higher batting average: .3429 to Williams's .3427, one ten-thousandth of a point higher . . . October 4: Joe DiMaggio becomes the first major leaguer to appear on the cover of *Time* magazine twice: his first time was on July 13, 1936, during his rookie season . . . Stan Musial of the Cardinals misses winning the NL Triple Crown by one rained-out home run. He led the NL in batting (.376) and RBIs (131), but lost the home run crown to Ralph Kiner and Johnny Mize who tied with 40, one more than Musial's 39.

Boudreau managed his Indians to a 4–2 World Series victory over the Boston Braves—Cleveland's first world championship since 1920. The Braves hadn't been in the World Series since the "Miracle Braves" swept in 1914. Boudreau is the only manager to win a World Series and be named the league's Most Valuable Player in the same season. More than 86,000 fans pack Cleveland Stadium for Game 5. ⚾

WHO'S WHO in BASEBALL

1950
THIRTY-FIFTH
EDITION

MEL PARNELL

PRICE
30c

35c. in Canada

1950—MEL PARNELL

The 1949 Boston Red Sox finished the season just one game behind their arch-rivals, the New York Yankees, but Mel Parnell, their star pitcher, had a great season. He's one of the few eligible players, including Paul Trout, Bucky Walters, Jim Konstanty, Hank Sauer, Bobby Shantz, and Eddie Dyer, to appear on the cover of *Who's Who in Baseball* who did *not* wind up in the Baseball Hall of Fame.

Parnell enlisted in the Army Air Corps during World War II, where he trained pilots. He was discharged as a staff sergeant.

In 1949, only his third big-league season, Parnell was the best pitcher in the American League. He led the majors with 25 wins—breaking Babe Ruth's single-season Red Sox record of 24, which had stood since 1917—was second in the AL with an ERA of 2.77, and led in both complete games (27), and innings pitched (295.1). Parnell gave up the fewest home runs per nine innings of all AL pitchers. He finished seventh in the American League with 122 strikeouts. (Virgil Trucks of the Detroit Tigers led with 153.) Parnell also walked 134 batters, setting a Red Sox record. Parnell was an All-Star and finished fourth in MVP voting, behind teammate Ted Williams.

To capture the AL pennant in 1949, the Red Sox had to win either of their final games of the season against the Yankees, October 1 and 2 in New York. Parnell pitched four innings in the first game but the Yankees won both and the AL pennant.

Parnell spent his entire 10-year career with the Red Sox. He won more games and pitched more innings than any other Red Sox lefty. His career 71-30 record at Fenway disproves the notion that lefties cannot win there. Parnell threw a 4–0 no-hitter at Fenway against the White Sox on July 14, 1956, the first Red Sox no-hitter since Howard Ehmke's in 1923.

Following his playing career, Parnell managed in the minors, did television broadcasts for the Red Sox from 1965 to 1968, and owned a pest-control business.

Only three pitchers won more games for the Red Sox than Mel Parnell's 123: Cy Young, Roger Clemens, and Tim Wakefield.

In and Around Baseball 1949:

Stan Musial was on the cover of *Time* magazine's September 5 issue . . . The entire St. Louis Cardinals team steals a total of 17 bases, the all-time National League low . . . DiMaggio hits safely in 34 straight games—the Boston Red Sox's *Dom* DiMaggio—the longest AL streak since brother Joe's 56 in 1941.

The New York Yankees beat the Brooklyn Dodgers 4–1 in the World Series, their first of an unmatched five consecutive world championships. 1949 is also the first of 10 straight years in which the World Series is played in New York City.

WHO'S WHO in BASEBALL

1951
THIRTY-SIXTH
EDITION

JIM KONSTANTY

PRICE
30c

(35c in Canada)

1951—JIM KONSTANTY

Casimir "Jim" Konstanty, from Strykersville, New York, was the first relief pitcher to appear on the cover of *Who's Who in Baseball*. A US Navy veteran with a master's degree in biology, he was an All-Star in 1950 for the Philadelphia Phillies and was the first relief pitcher to win the Most Valuable Player Award. He appeared in 74 games to lead both leagues, and saved 22—the most in the majors—without a start. *The Sporting News* named him their National League Pitcher of the Year.

Konstanty's palmball and slider helped the Phillies win their first pennant since 1916. But they were swept 4–0 in the World Series by the New York Yankees. Konstanty pitched in three games and lost Game 1.

In and Around Baseball 1950:

April 18: Opening Day is Opening Night, as the St. Louis Cardinals become the first team to start their season with a night game . . . August 31: Brooklyn Dodgers slugger Gil Hodges hits four homers in a game against the Boston Braves . . . Dom DiMaggio of the Boston Red Sox leads the American League with a grand total of 15 stolen bases—the lowest total for the league-leader ever . . . New York Yankees shortstop Phil Rizzuto bats .334 and wins the AL Most Valuable Player Award and the Hickok Belt for the best professional athlete.

Although they had led by 7½ games, by September 20, the Phillies lead over the Brooklyn Dodgers had shrunk to just 1. In the final game, Dick Sisler hits a three-run homer and Robin Roberts retires the Dodgers in the 10th. The 1950 Phillies—called "The Whiz Kids" because of their youth—were in the World Series, their first since 1915. But the Yankees swept them for their second consecutive world championship. 🌑

1952 • 50 CENTS IN CANADA • 37th EDITION
NEW AND ENLARGED

who's who in

STAN MUSIAL

BASEBALL

Edited By

JOSEPH LILLY

Editor, BASEBALL MAGAZINE

PUBLISHED BY

BASEBALL MAGAZINE COMPANY

1952—STAN MUSIAL

Stan "The Man" Musial was selected to 24 All-Star Games (there were two from 1959 to 1962), an unbreakable record he shares with Willie Mays and Hank Aaron.

1952 was Musial's second appearance on the cover of *Who's Who in Baseball*. His first was in 1944. He won the National League Most Valuable Player Awards in 1943 and again in 1946 and 1948. In 1951, Musial hit .355 and won the NL batting crown to go with 32 home runs (tied for fourth in the NL behind Ralph Kiner's 42) and a majors-leading 355 total bases. His St. Louis Cardinals finished third in the NL, behind the New York Giants.

Musial was second to Dodgers catcher Roy Campanella in MVP voting.

In and Around Baseball 1951:

July 12 and September 28: New York Yankees pitcher Allie Reynolds—"The Superchief"—became the first American League pitcher to throw two no-hitters in the same season . . . August 19: The greatest stunt in baseball history: In the bottom of the first inning, 3'7" Eddie Gaedel of the St. Louis Browns—wearing uniform number "1/8"—walks on four straight pitches. He is lifted for a pinch runner . . . September 20: NL president Ford C. Frick is unanimously elected commissioner of baseball.

All playoff games are special, but this one was extraordinary. For the first time, two National League teams *in the same city*—the Brooklyn Dodgers and the New York Giants—finished the season tied for first place with identical 97-59 records. The winner of the three-game playoff would go to the World Series. The Giants won Game 1 and the Dodgers won Game 2. The deciding Game 3 at the Polo Grounds is the first game to be telecast from coast to coast. It went into the bottom of the ninth inning. With two men on base and the Dodgers nursing a 4–2 lead, Ralph Branca, wearing #13, came in to pitch in relief of Don Newcombe. The batter: Glasgow-born Bobby Thomson. He blasted Branca's 2-0 pitch into the second deck down the left field line. Thomson's home run—perhaps the most famous in baseball history—has its own name: The "Shot Heard 'Round The World." The Giants won the pennant 5–4.

In the World Series, the Yankees beat the Giants 4–2.

1953 · 50 CENTS · 55c IN CANADA · 38th EDITION

who's who

in

BASEBALL

PUBLISHED BY

BASEBALL MAGAZINE COMPANY

SID FEDER, Editor

1953—HANK SAUER, BOBBY SHANTZ

In 1952, the 35-year-old Hank Sauer, a World War II veteran of the US Coast Guard, tied Ralph Kiner for the National League home run crown with 37. Sauer became the first major leaguer to homer three times off the same pitcher twice. He led the league with 121 RBIs and 71 extra base hits. Sauer was second in total bases and fourth in doubles.

Sauer was an All-Star and was voted the league's Most Valuable Player, edging out such perennial standouts (and future Hall of Famers) as Robin Roberts, Hoyt Wilhelm, Stan Musial, Enos Slaughter, Jackie Robinson, Pee Wee Reese, Duke Snider, Roy Campanella, and Red Schoendienst. Sauer was the first MVP from a second-division team. His Chicago Cubs finished the season in fifth place, 19½ games behind the first-place Brooklyn Dodgers.

Sauer had a 15-year major league career mostly as an outfielder for the Cubs, Reds, Giants, and Cardinals.

Bobby Shantz, one of the few players who threw left but batted righty, had a career year in 1952. Shantz, a 5'6", 139-pound hurler who threw a knuckleball and an excellent curveball, led the National League in 1952 with 24 wins—his career high—with only seven losses. His .774 winning percentage for the Philadelphia Athletics earned him an All-Star berth and the American League's Most Valuable Player Award. He was second in complete games, third in strikeouts and ERA, tied for third in shutouts, and fourth in innings pitched. Despite Shantz's outstanding season, the A's finished in fourth place.

On September 23, 1952—five days before the end of the season—Senators pitcher Walt Masterson broke Shantz's left wrist with a fastball.

Shantz spent the first six years of his 16-year career with the Philadelphia Athletics. He later pitched for six other teams. He was 0-1 in his two World Series appearances with the Yankees.

In and Around Baseball 1952:

April 15, Opening Day: Four umpires becomes the standard for regular season games . . . Topps issues its first set of baseball cards.

The New York Yankees win their fourth World Series in a row, beating their crosstown rivals, the Brooklyn Dodgers, 4–3.

1954 • 50 CENTS • 39th EDITION

who's who in

AL ROSEN

BASEBALL

PUBLISHED BY

BASEBALL MAGAZINE COMPANY

ALLAN ROTH, *Editor*

1954—AL ROSEN

Al "Flip" Rosen was known as a hard-nosed third baseman. Literally. An amateur boxer, Rosen's nose was broken 13 times. He was the first third baseman to appear on the cover of *Who's Who in Baseball*.

Rosen served in the US Navy from 1942 to 1946 and saw action in Okinawa. He was discharged as a lieutenant.

Rosen spent his entire 10-year career, 1947–1956, with the Cleveland Indians.

In 1950, he hit 37 home runs, a rookie record which stood until broken by Mark McGwire's 49 in 1987.

Rosen was a four-time All-Star, and was the unanimous American League Most Valuable Player in 1953—the first unanimous choice since Hank Greenberg in 1935. He was also *The Sporting News* Major League Player of the Year. Rosen led the AL with a personal-best 43 home runs and 145 RBIs. He also scored 115 runs. That year the Indians finished in second place, 8½ games behind the first place Yankees.

After his playing career, Rosen became a stockbroker and later a very successful front-office executive.

In and Around Baseball 1953:

After 76 years in Boston, the National League franchise known first as the Red Stockings, then the Beaneaters, the Doves, and finally the Braves, moves to Milwaukee, and plays its first game there in 1953. But the team stays in Milwaukee only 13 years, before moving to Atlanta in 1966 . . . May 6: St. Louis Browns pitcher Alva "Bobo" Holloman does something nobody has ever done before or since: In his first major league start, he throws a no-hitter to beat the Philadelphia Athletics 6–0 . . . June 18: During a 48-minute seventh inning, 23 Boston Red Sox bat and score 17 runs. Gene Stephens had three hits—a double and two singles.

By defeating the Brooklyn Dodgers 4–2 in the World Series, the New York Yankees did something that has not been done before or since: They won their fifth consecutive world championship.

50¢   1955   40th EDITION

who's who

in

AL   DARK

BASEBALL

PUBLISHED BY

Who's Who in Baseball Magazine Co., Inc.

ALLAN ROTH, Editor

1955—AL DARK

Alvin Dark—"The Swamp Fox"—was born in Comanche, Oklahoma. After bouts of malaria and diphtheria as a child, he became a standout athlete in college in baseball, basketball, and football. He was drafted by the Philadelphia Eagles. Dark served as an officer in the Marines in World War II, stationed in China.

Dark, the National League's Rookie of the Year in 1948 with the Boston Braves—after just one year in the minors—was the first winner of the Lou Gehrig Memorial Award in 1954 given by Phi Delta Theta, Gehrig's college fraternity, to the player who best exemplifies Gehrig's character. He hit a respectable .293 with 20 home runs for the New York Giants, and led the National League with 644 at-bats. He also led in two categories nobody wants to lead in: outs made (491) and errors (36).

Dark was the starting shortstop in the 1954 All-Star Game. In his seventh year in the majors, he played shortstop in all 154 games.

Dark was the first man to manage All-Star teams for both leagues—the National in 1963 and the American in 1975.

In and Around Baseball 1954:

The Major League Baseball Players Association is formed . . . At the height of the anticommunist scare, the Cincinnati Reds change their name to the "Redlegs." They switch back in 1960 . . . In the first American League franchise shift since 1902, the St. Louis Browns (perennial also-rans in the AL, except for 1944) move to Baltimore to become the Orioles . . . Willie Mays of the New York Giants might have earned a spot on the cover of *Who's Who in Baseball*: He led the National League batting .341 with 110 RBIs and 41 homers. He won the Most Valuable Player Award and the Hickok Belt . . . July 31: Joe Adcock of the Milwaukee Braves slugs four home runs against the Brooklyn Dodgers . . . August 13: Hank Aaron makes his big-league debut as the Milwaukee Braves open the season against the Reds in Cincinnati—the first game in which outfielders did not leave their gloves on the field between innings.

Willie Mays made the most famous catch in baseball history during the 1954 World Series—so famous, in fact, that it is known to this day simply as "The Catch." The Series pitted the AL Champion Cleveland Indians against Mays's New York Giants. In the top of the eighth inning of Game 1 at the Polo Grounds, with the score tied at two and runners on first and second, Vic Wertz hit a fly ball to the base of the wall in right-center field. Mays made an incredible over-the-shoulder basket catch, turned, and fired the ball to second base to prevent the runners from advancing. The Giants won the game 5–2. Alvin Dark hits .412 in the Series, as the Giants sweep the Indians, winners of 111 games in the regular season.

50¢　1956　41st EDITION

who's who in BASEBALL

DUKE　SNIDER

PUBLISHED BY
Who's Who in Baseball Magazine Co., Inc.
ALLAN ROTH Editor

1956—DUKE SNIDER

Edwin "Duke" Snider—"The Duke of Flatbush"— spent the first 16 years of his 18-year career as a center fielder with the Brooklyn and Los Angeles Dodgers. In 1955, he hit .309 and smacked 42 home runs (fourth best in the National League) and led the majors with 136 RBIs and 126 runs scored, the third time in a row he had led in that stat. He also led the NL in extra base hits with 82. He was an All-Star (one of eight selections), *The Sporting News* National League Player of the Year, and was second in NL MVP voting behind team-mate Roy Campanella.

Snider hit at least 40 home runs five years in a row (1953–1956) and had the most home runs (326) and the most RBIs in the 1950s (1,031).

Snider retired with 407 career home runs. His uniform #4 was retired by the Dodgers and he was elected to the Baseball Hall of Fame in 1980.

In and Around Baseball 1955:

After 54 years in Philadelphia, the Athletics move to Kansas City . . . Mickey Mantle leads the American League with 37 home runs and 11 triples (tied) . . . Across town, the Giants' Willie Mays leads the National League with 51 home runs and 13 triples (tied) . . . No AL pitcher wins 20 games.

The 1955 World Series was a classic: For the sixth time in the previous 14 years, the New York Yankees face their crosstown rivals, the Brooklyn Dodgers. The Yankees had beaten the Dodgers in 1941, 1947, 1949, 1952, and 1953. But not this year.

In his fourth all–New York World Series, Duke Snider hits .320 with four home runs (he also hit four in 1952), as the Dodgers' "Boys of Summer" finally beat the Yankees 4–3, for Brooklyn's only world championship. Tired of saying "Wait 'til next year!," Dodger fans rejoice: "This *IS* next year!"

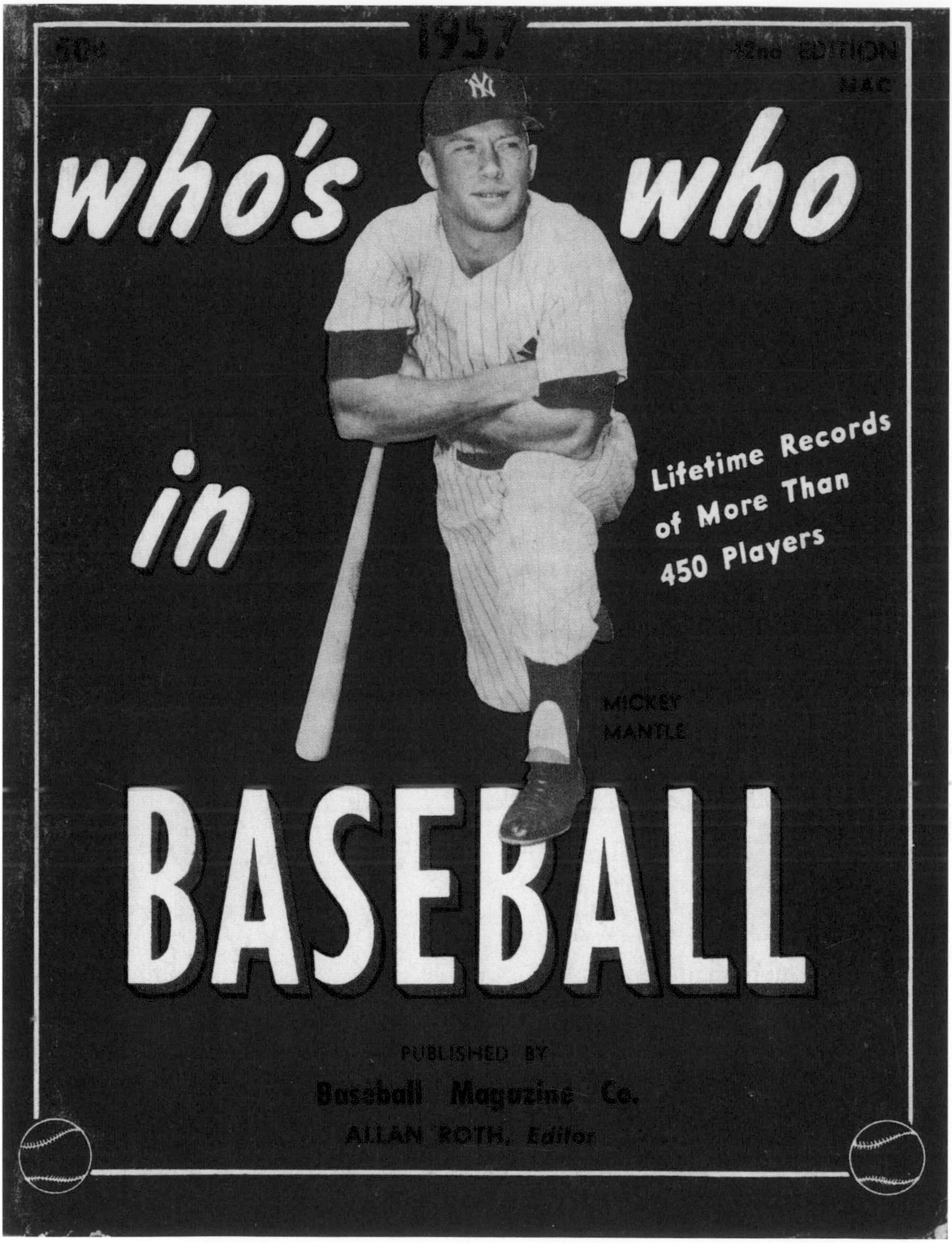

50¢
1957
42nd EDITION
MAC
who's who
in
Lifetime Records of More Than 450 Players
MICKEY MANTLE
BASEBALL
PUBLISHED BY
Baseball Magazine Co.
ALLAN ROTH, Editor

1957—MICKEY MANTLE

Mickey Mantle—"The Mick," from Spavinaw, Oklahoma—had many spectacular seasons with the New York Yankees.

At 19, Mantle was the youngest player in the American League in 1951, his rookie season when he shared the outfield with Joe DiMaggio, then in his final season.

Mantle was the greatest switch hitter ever, with power from both sides of the plate. He was also one of the best bunters in the league—a rare talent for a slugger. Mantle was among the fastest going to first on a hit—3.1 seconds.

Mantle was also an outstanding center fielder. Who knows what he might have accomplished if his career hadn't been marked by alcoholism and injuries? Toward the end of his life, Mantle said: "If I'd known I was going to live this long, I would have taken better care of myself."

In 1956, perhaps his most dominant season, he was the first Triple Crown winner since Ted Williams in 1947 with 130 RBIs, a .353 batting average, and 52 home runs—the most ever by a batting champion. Mantle led the AL in runs scored, extra base hits, reaching base, total bases, slugging percentage, and on-base percentage. He won his first of three AL Most Valuable Player awards, and was an All-Star (one of his 20 selections). He was also named *The Sporting News* Major League Player of the Year and won the Hickok Belt as the nation's best pro athlete.

Mantle hit 536 career home runs (including six inside-the parkers), third on the all-time list when he retired after the 1968 season, behind only Babe Ruth and Willie Mays. He hit 369 lefty and 167 righty. Mantle played in 65 World Series games, second only to Yogi Berra's incredible 75,

appearing in 12 World Series and on seven champion teams. He accomplished the rare feat of scoring more runs (1,676) than he drove in (1,509). Some of his World Series records may never be broken: 18 home runs, 26 extra base hits, 123 total bases, 40 RBIs, and 42 runs scored.

Mantle's #7 was retired by the Yankees, and he was elected to the Baseball Hall of Fame in 1974 with teammate Whitey Ford.

In and Around Baseball 1956:

April 19: The Brooklyn Dodgers play the first of 15 regular season games (1956–57) at Roosevelt Stadium in Jersey City, New Jersey, dropping a loud hint that they want to move . . . September 30: 16-year-old Jim Derrington pitches for the Chicago White Sox . . . Yankee Phil Rizzuto set a record which will never be broken: He plays in his 49th World Series game *in his hometown*—New York City . . . Willie Mays becomes the first 30-30 player in the National League with 36 home runs and 40 stolen bases. He does it again in 1957.

The World Series saw familiar rivals: for the sixth time in nine years, the New York Yankees faced the Brooklyn Dodgers. On October 8, in Game 5, the Yankees Don Larsen, who had an 11-5 record during the regular season, took the hill. Twenty-seven Dodgers came to the plate. None reached first base as Larsen pitched the only perfect game in World Series history—perhaps the greatest game ever pitched—before 64,519 fans at Yankee Stadium. Larsen's was the first perfect game in 34 years. He was named the Series Most Valuable Player. The Yankees won four games to Brooklyn's three to win the championship. 🌑

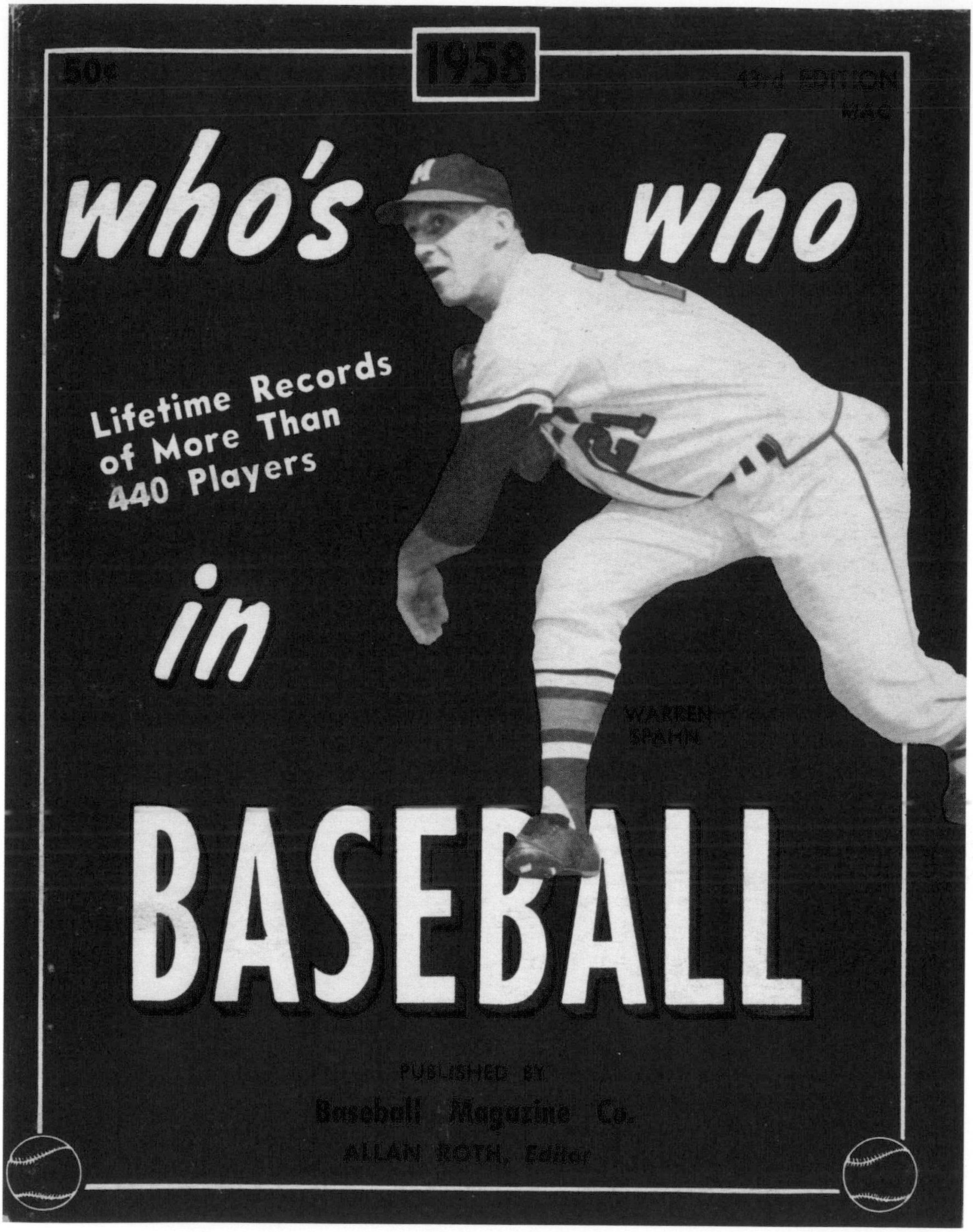
50¢
1958
43rd EDITION
who's who
Lifetime Records of More Than 440 Players
in
WARREN SPAHN
BASEBALL
PUBLISHED BY
Baseball Magazine Co.
ALLAN ROTH, Editor

1958—WARREN SPAHN

Warren Spahn didn't win his first major league game until he was 25. Because of a high school football injury, Spahn was unable to raise his right hand above his shoulder. He pitched left-handed in the majors for 21 seasons and won 363 games, losing only 245. Spahn won more games than any other left-handed pitcher. Only Cy Young (511), Walter Johnson (417), Christy Mathewson and Grover Cleveland Alexander (tied at 373) won more games. He was 39 when he threw his first no-hitter and 40 when he tossed his second.

Spahn knew his business. He said, "Hitting is timing. Pitching is upsetting timing." In 1957, Spahn led the National League with 21 wins for the Milwaukee Braves—the first of five consecutive titles—pitching 18 complete games. He was voted to the All-Star team (one of 14 selections) and won the Cy Young Award. He was *The Sporting News*'s National League Pitcher of the Year. (He won that again in 1958 and 1961.) His teammate Hank Aaron won the NL Most Valuable Player Award in 1957, making them the first teammates to win the Cy Young and the MVP Awards the same year.

Spahn did not play from 1943 to 1945 because he was in the US Army with the 276th Engineer Combat Battalion, 9th Armored Division in France. Wounded in both the Battle of the Bulge and the battle to hold the Bridge at Remagen, he was the only major leaguer to receive a battlefield commission: Sergeant Spahn became Lieutenant Spahn. He is the only ballplayer to earn a Bronze Star, the Army's fourth highest decoration in World War II. When he returned to the Braves in June 1946, he greeted manager Billy Southworth by saying: "This is the first time in years that I've reported to anybody without saluting."

Fifty years after his final game in 1965, Spahn still holds the career record for most home runs by a pitcher—35.

Spahn won at least 20 games 13 times and was 4-3 in three World Series. He was inducted into the Hall of Fame in 1973.

In and Around Baseball 1957:

Fans rather than managers or players picked the starters on the All-Star team in 1957. Thanks to a campaign by the Cincinnati *Enquirer* including pre-marked printed ballots, seven members of the Reds were elected to start for the National League: Wally Post, Gus Bell, Don Hoak, Roy McMillan, Johnny Temple, Ed Bailey, and Frank Robinson. Baseball commissioner Ford Frick appointed Hank Aaron and Willie Mays to join Stan Musial on the NL team. Post and Bell were out. Managers, players, and coaches selected the All-Stars until 1970, when the selections were returned to the fans, with a special panel reviewing the voting to prohibit stuffing the ballot box . . . June 12: Stan Musial of the St. Louis Cardinals plays in his 823rd consecutive game, breaking the previous National League record set by Gus Suhr . . . *The Sporting News* and Rawlings create the Gold Glove Award for the best defensive player at each position in each league.

The Milwaukee Braves beat the New York Yankees 4–3 in the World Series, the first Braves Fall Classic victory since the "Miracle" Boston Braves of 1914. 🌑

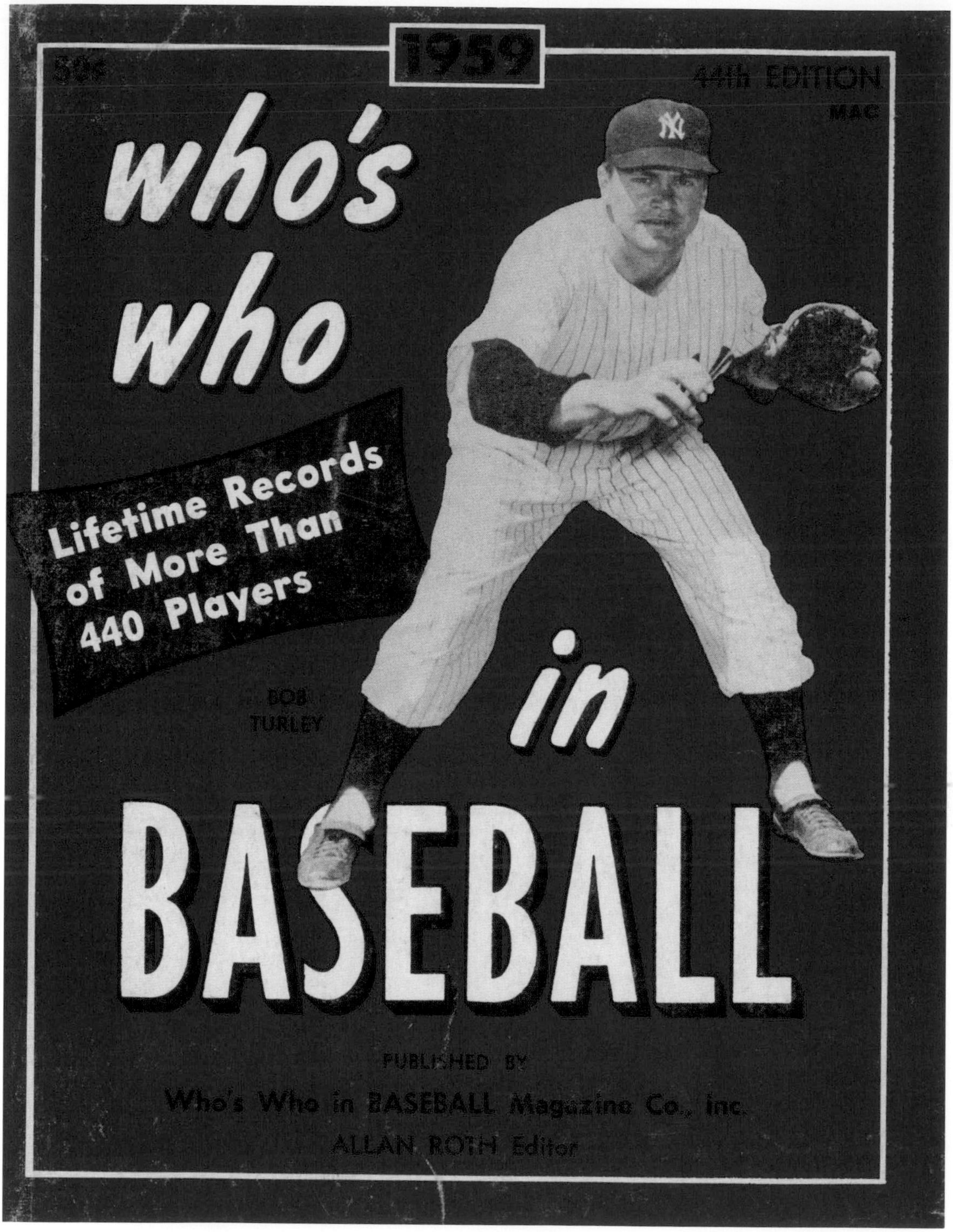
50¢
1959
44th EDITION
MAC
who's who
Lifetime Records of More Than 440 Players
BOB TURLEY
in
BASEBALL
PUBLISHED BY
Who's Who in BASEBALL Magazine Co., Inc.
ALLAN ROTH Editor

1959—BOB TURLEY

"Bullet" Bob Turley was a right-handed fastballer from Troy, Illinois. He was 21-7 in 1958 for the New York Yankees, leading the American League in wins, winning percentage, and complete games (19). Surprisingly, he also led the major leagues (for the third time) with 128 walks.

Turley was named to the AL All-Star team and won the Cy Young Award (only one award covered both leagues at the time). His fielding average was a perfect 1.000.

He was named *The Sporting News* American League Pitcher of the Year and Major League Player of the Year. He was second in MVP voting to the Red Sox's Jackie Jensen. Turley won the Hickok Belt in 1958 as the best professional athlete in the country.

Over his 12-year career, Turley pitched in 15 World Series games, all with the Yankees. He was in the Fall Classic four years in a row, 1955–1958. His postseason record was 4-3 with an ERA of 3.19. He retired after going 1-4 with the Boston Red Sox in 1963.

In and Around Baseball 1958:

January 28: 30-year-old Brooklyn Dodger All-Star Roy Campanella, the first black catcher in the majors, is paralyzed when his rented car skids on an icy road and hits a telephone pole near his New York home. The crash fractures his spinal cord. Campy never walks again . . . Baseball moves west. After 73 years in Brooklyn, the Dodgers move 3,000 miles west to Los Angeles. After 74 years in New York City, the Giants move too, to San Francisco. The first major league game on the West Coast is the *San Francisco* Giants vs. the *Los Angeles* Dodgers at San Francisco's Seals Stadium, April 15, 1958 . . . May 13: Stan Musial of the St. Louis Cardinals get his 3,000th career hit.

For an unmatched 10 consecutive years, at least part of the World Series is played in New York City. The 1958 Series matches the same two teams as in 1957. This year, the Yankees beat the Milwaukee Braves 4–3.

Turley was 2-1 in the World Series, pitching a shutout in Game 5 and winning Game 7. He was named the Series' Most Valuable Player.

50¢

45th EDITION

MAC

1960

who's who

Lifetime Records of More Than 470 Players

in
BASEBALL

DON DRYSDALE

PUBLISHED BY

Baseball Magazine Co.

ALLAN ROTH Editor

1960—DON DRYSDALE

Don Drysdale threw an intimidating sidearm fastball. The 6'5" right-hander had a 14-year Hall of Fame career, all with the Brooklyn and Los Angeles Dodgers. He was known as much for his strikeouts—he led the National League in Ks three times, and struck out over 200 six times—as for hit batsman: he led the NL in that stat five times.

In 1959, he led the National League with four shutouts and 242 strikeouts. He struck out almost one batter per inning, tops in the NL. He also hit the most batters—18. Drysdale pitched in eight All-Star Games, including 1959.

He led his Dodgers to their first world championship in Los Angeles in 1959, a 4–2 win over the Chicago White Sox. Drysdale was also a member of Dodger champion teams in 1963 and 1965.

Drysdale was a workhorse. He led the league in innings pitched twice, and he smacked seven home runs in a season twice, once batting .300. But a sore shoulder forced his retirement after the 1969 season. He was only 32.

In the 1960s, Drysdale and teammate Sandy Koufax were the dominant pitching pair in the National League. In 1962, Drysdale won the Cy Young Award as the best pitcher in the major leagues.

Drysdale started five All-Star Games and still holds the record for most All-Star Game innings pitched (1/3) and most All-Star Game strikeouts (19).

In 1968, Drysdale broke Walter Johnson's 55-year-old record of 55 2/3 consecutive scoreless innings pitched by throwing 58 consecutive scoreless innings. That record stood for 20 years until it was broken. Drysdale's mark was broken by another Dodger; Orel Hershiser, with 59 consecutive scoreless innings pitched in 1988.

After his playing career, Drysdale became a broadcaster for the Expos, Rangers, Angels, White Sox, and Dodgers. Drysdale was inducted into the Baseball Hall of Fame in 1984. Drysdale is the only Hall of Famer married to a Hall of Famer. His wife, Ann Meyers, is in the Basketball Hall of Fame.

Forty-six years after he retired, Drysdale still holds the record of most batters hit in a career—154.

In and Around Baseball 1959:

May 7: The largest crowd ever to see a major league game—93,103—turns out for an exhibition game with the New York Yankees at the Los Angeles Coliseum (converted to baseball while Dodger Stadium is built) for "Roy Campanella Night" . . . May 26: In one of the greatest games ever played, 5'9" Pittsburgh Pirates pitcher Harvey "Kitten" Haddix was perfect for 12 innings, retiring 36 Milwaukee Brave batters in a row—a record which still stands. But Pittsburgh didn't score either and Haddix lost the game 1–0. In the 13th inning, Felix Mantilla reached on an error and was sacrificed to second. Hank Aaron was intentionally walked. Then Joe Adcock hit a home run into the stands, driving Mantilla home. But Adcock passed Aaron on the basepaths. The winning run counted, but Adcock's homer was later ruled a double . . . June 10: Cleveland Indians slugger Rocky Colavito smacks four home runs in a game against the Baltimore Orioles . . . July 21: 12 years after Jackie Robinson broke baseball's color line, Elijah "Pumpsie" Green made his debut at second base with the Red Sox, making Boston the last team to have a black player.

The 1959 World Series was the first one with a West Coast team—the Los Angeles Dodgers. They beat the Chicago White Sox 4–2.

50¢ · 1961 · 46th EDITION

MAC

who's
who

Lifetime Records
of More Than
470 Players

in
BASEBALL

ROGER
MARIS

PUBLISHED BY

Who's Who in Baseball Magazine Company, Inc.

ALLAN ROTH Editor

1961—ROGER MARIS

After four seasons with the Cleveland Indians and the Kansas City Athletics, Roger Maris was part of an eight-player trade late in 1959 that brought him to the New York Yankees for the 1960 season.

Maris, only 25, led the American League with 112 RBIs and a slugging percentage of .581. His Yankee teammate Mickey Mantle led the AL with 40 home runs, but Maris was right behind with 39—more than double his output of the previous year. His efforts earned him his second of four All-Star selections and a Gold Glove in right field. In the closest voting ever for Most Valuable Player, Maris beat Mantle by three points. Maris and Mantle were one of the most potent one-two punches in baseball history. The Yankees drew over 1.6 million fans in 1960 and won the pennant, finishing eight games ahead of the Baltimore Orioles.

The following season, Maris, an excellent right fielder, and teammate Mantle—known as "The M & M Boys"—battled all season for the home run crown. Most Yankee fans were rooting for Mantle, who had never played for any other team, but he had a late-season injury. Maris won it with 61, breaking Babe Ruth's record of 60, set in 1927.

Maris, a very reticent person, did not care for the media circus that surrounded his every move with the Yankees. His hair started to fall out. After seven seasons in New York, he finished his career with two years with the St. Louis Cardinals. He never again approached his titanic achievement of 1961.

Maris hit six home runs in seven World Series, including five in a row with the Yankees. He appeared in 41 World Series games.

In and Around Baseball 1960:

The Chicago White Sox become the first team to put players' names on their backs . . . April 17: The Cleveland Indians trade 1959 home run champ Rocky Colavito to the Detroit Tigers for 1959 batting champ Harvey Kuenn . . . September 5: At age 41, relief pitcher Diomedes Olivo makes his major league debut with the Pittsburgh Pirates. He's the oldest rookie in the history of the National League . . . September 28: Ted Williams comes to bat in the bottom of the eighth inning at Boston's Fenway Park. It was Boston's last home game of the season. Baltimore led 4–2. Williams was not going to make the team's last road trip to New York. Baltimore's Jack Fisher delivered the pitch. Williams smacked it into the right field seats—his 521st and final career home run. He circled the bases and ran into the Boston dugout. His career was over . . . The last Negro League plays its final season.

The New York Yankees finished the season in first place. In the World Series, they faced the Pittsburgh Pirates. Through the first six games, the Yankees had outscored the Pirates 55–26, but that didn't matter in Game 7. In the bottom of the ninth inning, the deciding game was tied at 9. Second baseman Bill Mazeroski faced Yankee reliever Bill Terry. Mazeroski hit a 1-1 pitch into the left field stands for the only seventh game walk-off home run to decide a World Series. Mazeroski rode that home run into the Hall of Fame. 🔵

50¢

1962

47th EDITION

MAC

ED
"WHITEY"
FORD

who's who

Lifetime Records of More Than 525 Players

in

BASEBALL

PUBLISHED BY
Who's Who in Baseball Magazine Company, Inc.
ALLAN ROTH Editor

1962—WHITEY FORD

Edward "Whitey" Ford—"The Chairman of the Board"—spent his entire 16-year career with his hometown New York Yankees, with two years (1951 and 1952) out for military service. Coincidentally, Ford wore #16, which the Yankees later retired for him. Ford became the dominant pitcher of his era. His career record was 236-106, with a winning percentage of .690, third best all time.

1961 was a great year for the Yankees. Mickey Mantle hit 54 home runs, and Roger Maris hit a historic 61. Elston Howard, Bill "Moose" Skowron, and Yogi Berra each hit over 20 homers. The team turned a league-leading 500 double plays. Maris was the MVP. They finished the season 109-53.

Ford had a career year in 1961. He won 25 and lost only four games, to lead the American League in wins and winning percentage (.862). He also led the league with 283 innings pitched—a career high. He had three shutouts and 11 complete games. Ford was elected to the All-Star team, was the Most Valuable Player in the World Series (2-0, one shutout, 14 scoreless innings), and won the Cy Young Award.

Forty-eight years after he retired, Ford still holds the World Series records for games started (22), wins (10), losses (8), innings pitched (146), strikeouts (94), and walks (34). He pitched 33 consecutive scoreless World Series innings.

In and Around Baseball 1961:

April 11: The Chicago Cubs open the season without a manager: a "College of Coaches" runs the team all season. Badly. The Cubs finish 64-90, in seventh place . . . April 19: Responding to complaints that fans couldn't see over the vendors at Chicago's Comiskey Park, White Sox owner Bill Veeck—the greatest showman and promoter in baseball history—hires eight midgets to work the box seats for the White Sox home opener . . . April 30: Willie Mays of the San Francisco Giants hits four home runs against the Milwaukee Braves . . . July 11: In the first All-Star Game of the year, Stu Miller of the Giants relieves Sandy Koufax in the ninth inning at San Francisco's Candlestick Park, Miller's home park. Roger Maris is on first and Al Kaline on second when Miller is blown off the mound by Candlestick's infamous winds. A balk is called, and the runners move up. The NL wins 5–4 . . . July 31: The second 1961 All-Star Game at Boston's Fenway Park was the first to end in a tie when rain prevented the game, tied at 1, from going into extra innings . . . The Senators, a Washington, DC franchise since 1901, move to Minnesota and become the Twins in 1961. A second Washington American League franchise, also called the Senators, played its first game in 1961. In 1972 they moved to Arlington to become the Texas Rangers . . . October 1, the last day of the season: Roger Maris hits his 61st home run for the New York Yankees, breaking the most famous record in sports: Babe Ruth's 60 home runs set in 1927. During all of 1961, Maris (who batted ahead of Mickey Mantle) did not receive a single intentional walk.

The New York Yankees were world champions for the 19th time in 1961, defeating the Cincinnati Reds 4–1.

60¢

48th EDITION

MAC

1963

who's who

Lifetime Records
of More Than
500 Players

DON DRYSDALE

in

BASEBALL

PUBLISHED BY
Who's Who in Baseball Magazine Company, Inc.

ALLAN ROTH Editor

1963—DON DRYSDALE

Don Drysdale of the Los Angeles Dodgers was back on the cover of *Who's Who in Baseball* three years after his first appearance.

In 1962, "Big D" won 25 games—the most in his career—and struck out 232 batters, the third time he had led in that category. He was an All-Star and won the Cy Young Award. But the Dodgers were second by one game to their rivals, the San Francisco Giants.

The season Willie Mays of the San Francisco Giants had in 1962 might have earned him a *Who's Who in Baseball* cover. He hit .304, smashed a league's best 49 home runs, collected 382 total bases, and drove in 141 runs—his career high. Mays also stole 18 bases. Mays's efforts made him the highest paid player in baseball in 1963: He earned a reported $105,000.

In and Around Baseball 1962:

Expansion: Four years after the Dodgers and the Giants moved to California, New York gets a new National League team—the hapless (120 losses) but lovable Mets. Houston also gets a new NL team—the Colt .45's, who later changed their name to the Astros. In the American League, the Los Angeles Angels (later the California Angels, Anaheim Angels, and most recently, the Los Angeles Angels of Anaheim) enter the league, owned by the singing cowboy Gene Autry . . . Maury Wills of the Los Angeles Dodgers stole 104 bases, breaking Ty Cobb's record of 96 set in 1915 and was the National League's Most Valuable Player, edging Willie Mays. Wills won the 1962 Hickok Belt . . . April 26: The Cleveland Indians trade Harry Chiti to the New York Mets for a player to be named later. On June 15, the Mets name the player: Harry Chiti . . . September 12: Tom Cheney of the Washington Senators strikes out 21 batters in a 16-inning game . . . Bob Buhl, a pitcher for the Milwaukee Braves and the Chicago Cubs, goes 0-for-1962 at the plate: 85 plate appearances, no hits.

The Yankees met the Giants for the seventh time in the World Series, but for the first time since they were the *San Francisco* Giants. A thrilling Game 7 ended when, with the Yankees up 1–0, Matty Alou on third, and Willie Mays on second representing the winning run, Willie McCovey lined a hard smash to second baseman Bobby Richardson to end the game and the series. 🏐

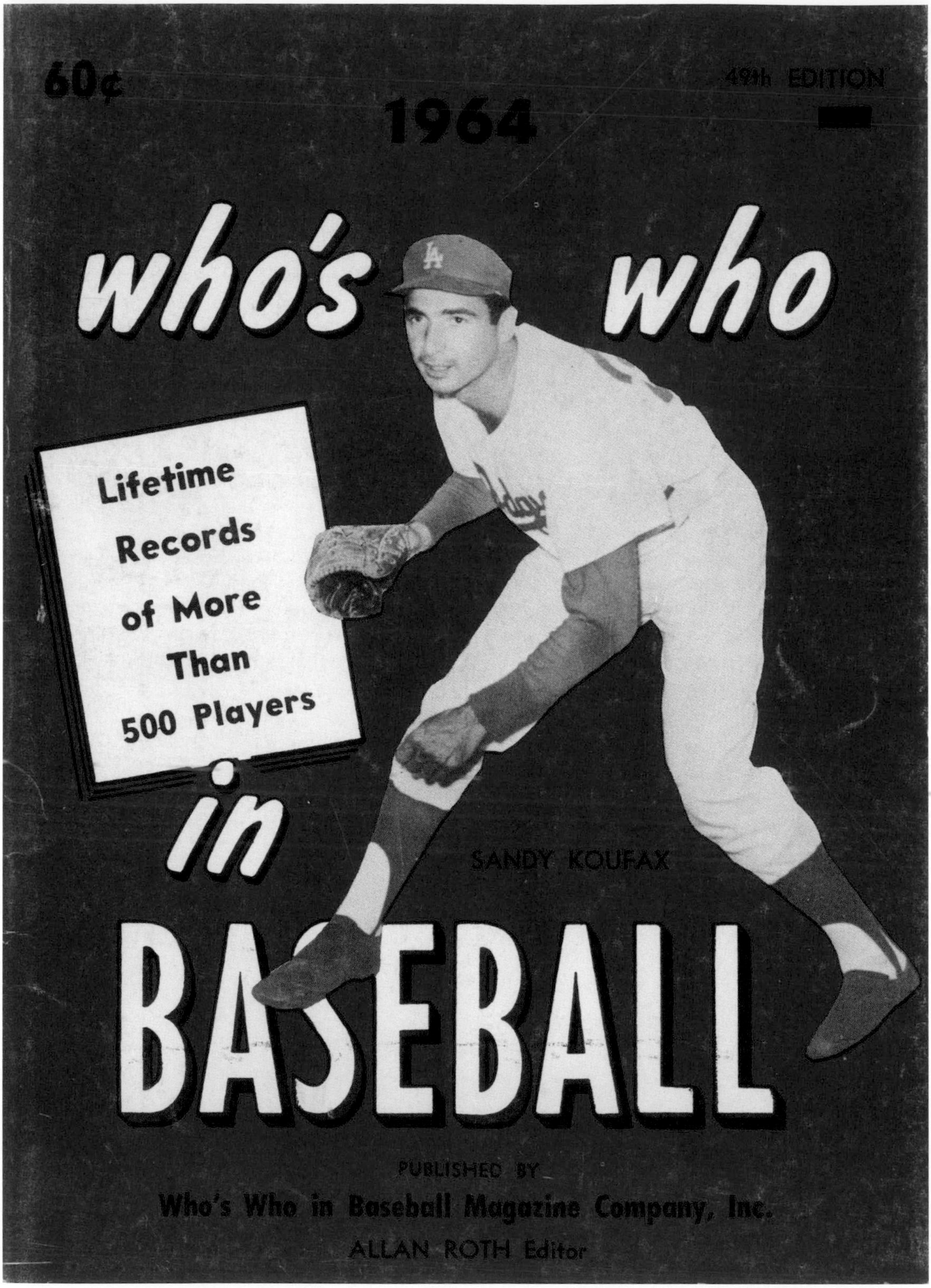

60¢

49th EDITION

1964

who's who

Lifetime
Records
of More
Than
500 Players

in

SANDY KOUFAX

BASEBALL

PUBLISHED BY

Who's Who in Baseball Magazine Company, Inc.

ALLAN ROTH Editor

1964—SANDY KOUFAX

Between 1962 and 1966 Sandy Koufax (born Sanford Braun) had five of the best years any pitcher has ever had. Pitching for the Los Angeles Dodgers, Koufax led the National League in ERA for five consecutive seasons. During that period, he also led the league in wins and in strikeouts three times. Fifty years later, his 382 strikeouts in 1965 is still the NL single-season record for left-handers. Only Nolan Ryan in the American League has struck out more in one season, 383 in 1973.

The 6'2" Koufax, who started his Dodger career in his native Brooklyn, went to the University of Cincinnati on a basketball scholarship. In 1963, Koufax rode his blazing fastball and devastating curve to the Triple Crown of Pitching with 25 victories—including 11 shutouts—while losing only 5!, 306 strikeouts, and an ERA of 1.88 in 311 innings. He was an All-Star and won both the Most Valuable Player and NL Cy Young Awards, his first of three. He also won the Hickok Belt as the nation's top professional athlete. Koufax won the Triple Crown of Pitching again in 1965 and 1966—the only man besides Walter Johnson and Grover Cleveland Alexander to win it three times.

Koufax was one of the worst batters in the history of the game, compiling a career .097 average and 28 total RBIs in 12 years. But he did manage to hit two home runs.

He struck out 18 in a game twice and pitched four no-hitters including a perfect game in 1965, the only game with only one hit. In four World Series appearances, the future Hall of Famer (at age 37, the youngest living inductee) had an ERA of 0.95.

He retired at 30, after the 1966 season in which he won the Cy Young Award for the third time, fearful of causing further injury to his arthritic left arm—one of the few great players to retire at the top of his game.

In and Around Baseball 1963:

June 23: After hitting the 100th home run of his career, Jimmy Piersall of the New York Mets circles the bases facing backwards . . . September 10: 42-year-old Stan Musial homers as his St. Louis Cardinals beat the Chicago Cubs 8–0. He's the first grandfather to homer in the big leagues. His first grandchild was born the night before . . . September 15: The three San Francisco Giant outfielders in the seventh inning are the Alou brothers: Felipe, Matty, and Jesus . . . September 27: The Houston Colt .45's (Astros) field an all-rookie lineup.

Sandy Koufax led the Dodgers to a 4–0 World Series sweep of the New York Yankees, and was named the Series MVP, an award he won again in 1965. 🏐

60¢

50th EDITION

1965

MAC

NEW! Lifetime Records Plus **PHOTOS** of More Than 500 Players

who's who

LARRY JACKSON

JOE TORRE

JUAN MARICHAL

TONY OLIVA

KEN BOYER

in

BASEBALL

PUBLISHED BY

Who's Who in Baseball Magazine Company, Inc.

ALLAN ROTH Editor

1965—KEN BOYER, LARRY JACKSON, JOE TORRE, JUAN MARICHAL, TONY OLIVA

For the first time, the 1965 edition of *Who's Who in Baseball* included more than two players—five, in fact—on its cover.

During his 15 seasons in the majors (Cardinals, Mets, Dodgers, White Sox), Kenton "Ken" Boyer, one of 14 children, was one of the best third basemen in the game. He won five Gold Gloves.

In 1964, with the St. Louis Cardinals, he hit 24 home runs (he hit exactly 24 home runs for four years in a row) and led the National League with 119 RBIs. He was an All-Star (one of seven selections), and was named *The Sporting News* Major League Player of the Year and the NL Most Valuable Player.

Boyer hit two homers as the Cardinals beat the Yankees in the World Series—their first title in 18 years—where he was opposed by his brother Clete, on the Yankees. (Another brother, Cloyd, had a five-year major league career.) For the first time ever, two brothers both homered in the Series. Only the Canseco, Aaron, and DiMaggio brothers hit more combined home runs than the Boyers. When he retired in 1969, only Stan Musial had hit more home runs for the Cardinals (475) than Ken Boyer (275). In 1984, the Cardinals retired his #14—the only Cardinal who is not a Hall of Famer to be so honored.

Larry Jackson, the only player in baseball history from Nampa, Idaho, pitched in the majors for 14 seasons. In 1964, with the Chicago Cubs, he led the National League with 24 wins and 85 assists and was the best-fielding pitcher in the league, but the Cubs finished eighth in a ten-team league. After his playing career, he became an Idaho state legislator.

Before he was a Hall of Fame manager, Joe Torre was a standout player. Although he played over 700 games at first base and over 500 at third, Torre spent most of his 18-year career as a catcher. He retired as a player during the 1977 season with a career batting average of .297, 1,185 RBIs, and 252 career home runs.

In 1964, with the Milwaukee Braves, Torre was the best-fielding catcher in the National League. He hit .321 with 20 home runs and 109 RBIs and made his second of nine All-Star teams.

Juan Marichal was as well known for his high-kicking windup as for his dominance of batters. He retired in 1975, after 16 seasons in the majors, with 2,303 strikeouts and 243 wins. He was the first Dominican to grace the *Who's Who* cover, and was one of the first two Hispanic players to appear (with Tony Oliva the same year).

In 1964, he finished what he started. Pitching for the San Francisco Giants, he went 21-8—his 21 wins was second in the National League—and led the NL with 22 complete games—one of 10 times he had at least 14 complete games. He earned a spot on the All-Star team.

Although he was considered the best right-handed pitcher of the 1960s, he never won a Cy Young Award. Marichal was the first Dominican elected to the Hall of Fame. His son-in-law José Rijo was the Most Valuable Player of the 1990 World Series with the Reds. After he retired, Marichal became the Minister of Sports in the Dominican Republic.

In 1964, with the Minnesota Twins, 25-year-old rookie outfielder Tony (born Pedro) Oliva—the first Cuban to appear on the cover of *Who's Who in Baseball*—exploded onto the scene as he led the American League with a .323 batting average. In 1965, he became the first man to win the batting crown in his first two full seasons. He also led the AL with 109 runs scored, 217 hits, 84 extra base hits, 374 total bases, and 43 doubles. Oliva was also a top right fielder, leading the AL in putouts with 290, one of six times he led in that stat.

In 1964, Oliva was an All-Star (one of eight selections), and was named American League Rookie of the Year.

In and Around Baseball 1964:

June 21, Father's Day: In the first game of a doubleheader, Philadelphia Phillies pitcher Jim Bunning throws a perfect game against the New York Mets at Shea Stadium. It's the first perfect game in the National League in 84 years. Bunning later served as a Republican US senator from Kentucky . . . September 1: Masanori Murakami, the first big-league player from Japan, debuts with the San Francisco Giants.

In the World Series, Bob Gibson pitched in three games (two complete), struck out 31 in 27 innings, and went 2-1 as his St. Louis Cardinals beat the New York Yankees 4–3. Gibson was the World Series Most Valuable Player. 🎾

60¢   MAC   51st EDITION

1966

WILLIE MAYS

SAM McDOWELL

SANDY KOUFAX

Lifetime Records
Plus **PHOTOS**
of More Than
500 Players

EDDIE FISHER

ZOILO VERSALLES

who's who
in BASEBALL

PUBLISHED BY

Who's Who in Baseball Magazine Company, Inc.

ALLAN ROTH Editor

1966—SANDY KOUFAX, WILLIE MAYS, SAM MCDOWELL, EDDIE FISHER, ZOILO VERSALLES

In 1965, Los Angeles Dodgers pitcher Sandy Koufax won the Triple Crown of Pitching for the second time, leading *both* leagues—with 26 wins, an ERA of 2.04, and 382 strikeouts. Koufax has held the NL record for most strikeouts in a season for 50 years.

Koufax was an All-Star and won his second of three Cy Young Awards. On September 9, 1965, he threw a perfect game—the first by a lefty in more than 100 years—against the Chicago Cubs in Los Angeles.

In 1965, Willie Mays led the majors with 52 home runs. He had hit 51 in 1955 and averaged 36 home runs per season over his career and led the league with a slugging percentage of .645 and a .398 on-base percentage. He won his second National League Most Valuable Player Award, a Gold Glove, and was an All-Star. His San Francisco Giants won 95 games but still finished 2 games behind the Los Angeles Dodgers.

Because two All-Star Games were held from 1959 to 1962, Mays, Hank Aaron, and Stan Musial share a record which will probably stand forever: each was selected to play in 24 All-Star Games. Forty-two years after he retired, Mays still holds these career All-Star Game records: most at-bats (75), hits (23), stolen bases (6), runs scored (20), total bases (40, tied with Stan Musial), and triples (3, tied with Brooks Robinson).

He also hit 660 career home runs. When he retired, Mays was #2 on the all-time home run list—behind only Babe Ruth's 714.

Mays was the first African American to appear on the cover.

"Sudden" Sam McDowell's overpowering fastball helped him win 17 games for the Cleveland Indians with a league-leading ERA of 2.18 and 325 strikeouts. He was selected for the All-Star team. McDowell was an intimidating pitcher: the 6'5" southpaw led the league in strikeouts five times and wild pitches three times.

Eddie Fisher, a 6'2" knuckleballer who pitched for the Chicago White Sox in 1965, appeared in a league-leading 82 games and earned 24 saves with a 15-7 record and an ERA of 2.40. He was an All-Star.

Twenty-five-year-old Cuban native Zoilo Versalles had an outstanding year in 1965 for the Minnesota Twins: most runs scored (126), doubles (45), triples (12), plate appearances (728), and total bases (308) in the American League. The shortstop also led the league with 122 strikeouts. He was selected as an All-Star, won a Gold Glove, and was chosen the league's Most Valuable Player—the first foreign-born MVP.

Versalles led the Twins to their first American League pennant since 1933 (when they were the Washington Senators).

In and Around Baseball 1965:

To prevent rich teams (i.e., the New York Yankees) from signing whichever players they wanted to, the draft is instituted. April 28: For the only time ever, a baseball game is broadcast from fair territory, as Lindsey Nelson broadcasts a Mets-Astros game from a gondola suspended 208 feet above second base at "The Eighth Wonder of the World"—the Houston Astrodome . . . July 20: Yankees pitcher Mel Stottlemyre hits an inside-the-park grand slam . . . August 22: Juan Marichal is pitching as the Giants face Sandy Koufax of the Dodgers in San Francisco. Marichal had already knocked down two Dodgers. In the bottom of the third inning, Marichal comes up to the plate. When Dodger catcher Johnny Roseboro throws the ball back to Koufax, it hits Marichal's ear. He shouts at Roseboro, and as the catcher stands up to argue, Marichal hits him over the head with his bat. Both benches clear. Roseboro, still bleeding profusely, has to leave the game. Marichal is ejected, fined $1,750, and suspended for eight games . . . September 8: Bert Campaneris of the Oakland Athletics becomes the first man to play all nine positions in one game . . . General William D. "Spike" Eckert—sometimes disparagingly referred to as "The Unknown Soldier"—is unanimously elected as the fourth commissioner of baseball, succeeding Ford Frick.

In the World Series, the Los Angeles Dodgers face the Minnesota Twins, playing in their first postseason. On October 6, Dodger pitcher Sandy Koufax, who is Jewish, decides not to pitch in Game 1, played on Yom Kippur, the Day of Atonement. Don Drysdale pitches in his place and loses. But the Dodgers come back to win the Series 4–3.

60¢

52nd EDITION

1967

who's who
in BASEBALL

FRANK ROBINSON

SANDY KOUFAX

Lifetime Records
Plus **PHOTOS**
of More Than
500 Players

ROBERTO CLEMENTE

JIM KAAT

PUBLISHED BY
Who's Who in Baseball Magazine Company, Inc.
ALLAN ROTH Editor

1967—FRANK ROBINSON, SANDY KOUFAX, ROBERTO CLEMENTE, JIM KAAT

Frank Robinson was the National League's Rookie of the Year as a 20-year-old in 1956 with the Cincinnati Reds. He won the NL's Most Valuable Player Award in 1961, also with the Reds. But in December 1965, at age 30, Robinson was traded to the Baltimore Orioles. Reds general manager Bill DeWitt said he was "an *old* 30."

In 1966, Robinson had one of the best offensive seasons ever. On May 8, he hit the only fair ball ever hit out of Baltimore's Memorial Stadium. Robinson won the American League Triple Crown with a career-high 49 home runs, 122 RBIs, and a .316 batting average. He also led the league with 122 runs scored, 85 extra base hits, 367 total bases, a .637 slugging percentage, and a .410 on-base percentage. His fielding average was a league-leading .992 as a right fielder. Robinson was a 14-time All-Star.

He was the Most Valuable Player in the American League—the only man ever to be named MVP in both leagues. Robinson was also named the World Series MVP as his Orioles won their first World Series, a 4–0 sweep of the Dodgers. He was *The Sporting News*'s Major League Player of the Year.

When he retired, his 586 home runs put him #4 on the career list, behind only Hank Aaron, Babe Ruth, and Willie Mays.

Robinson became baseball's first black manager with Cleveland in 1975 and a Hall of Famer in 1982. His uniform #20 was retired by both the Reds and the Orioles.

Sandy Koufax became the first player to appear on the cover of *Who's Who in Baseball* three times (1964, 1966, and 1967). He retired at 30 after the 1966 season.

Koufax led the majors with 27 wins—a career high—an ERA of 1.73, and 317 strikeouts, to win the National League Triple Crown of Pitching for the second consecutive season, and the third time in four years. He won his third NL Cy Young Award and was an All-Star.

Roberto Clemente, a native of Puerto Rico, spent his entire 18-year major league career with the Pittsburgh Pirates. In 1966 Clemente batted .317, hit 29 home runs, and was second in the league with 71 extra base hits. He led the league with 17 assists from right field, won the Gold Glove (one of 12 consecutive), and was named the National League's Most Valuable Player.

Clemente won the NL batting title four times and was named to 14 All-Star teams. Clemente was the Most Valuable Player in the 1971 World Series. He was killed in the crash of his overloaded plane bringing relief supplies to earthquake-ravaged Managua, Nicaragua, on New Year's Eve 1972. He had exactly 3,000 hits. His uniform #21 was retired by the Pirates, and he was elected to the Baseball Hall of Fame the next year by acclamation.

Pitching for the Minnesota Twins in 1966, Jim "Kitty" Kaat, from Zeeland, Michigan, led the American League with 25 wins and 19 complete games, 304.2 innings pitched, and 1,227 batters faced. He also had the fewest walks per nine innings. He was an All-Star and a Gold Glove winner.

But Kaat came in fifth in Most Valuable Player voting behind Frank Robinson of the Baltimore Orioles. 1966 was the last year with just one Cy Young Award, and it went to Sandy Koufax of the Dodgers who was 27-9. Kaat's Twins finished second in the American League, behind the first place Orioles.

After pitching in the major leagues for 25 years—a record at the time—Kaat retired during the 1983 season having played during four decades with 283 wins and 18 saves. Kaat pitched like he was double-parked, getting the ball to the plate in fewer than 12 seconds after getting it. Kaat was also one of the best fielding pitchers ever. He won 16 Gold Gloves on the mound and hit 16 career home runs.

In and Around Baseball 1966:

After 13 seasons in Milwaukee (after a previous move from Boston), the Braves become the first team to move twice: they settle in Atlanta. Future Hall of Famer Eddie Mathews becomes the only man to play for one franchise in three cities . . . April 6: Emmett Ashford, the first black umpire, works his first game . . . July 3: Atlanta Braves pitcher Tony Cloninger connects for grand slams in the first and fourth innings against the San Francisco Giants. Cloninger finishes the day with nine RBIs . . . For the only time, brothers finished 1, 2 in the National League batting race: Matty Alou of the Pittsburgh Pirates hits .342 to win the crown. His brother Felipe, with the Atlanta Braves, finishes second with .327.

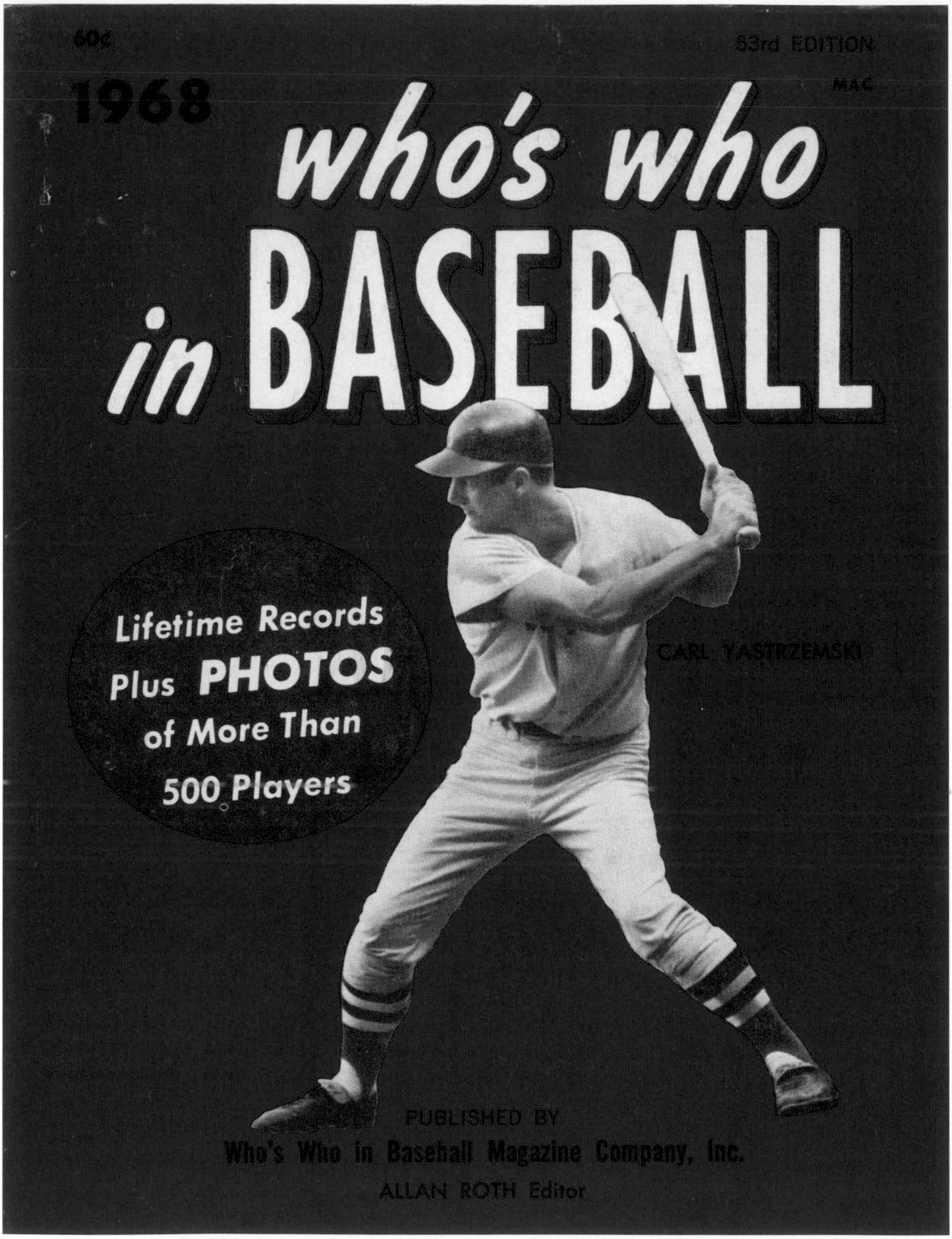

60¢

53rd EDITION

MAC

1968

who's who
in BASEBALL

**Lifetime Records
Plus PHOTOS
of More Than
500 Players**

CARL YASTRZEMSKI

PUBLISHED BY
Who's Who in Baseball Magazine Company, Inc.
ALLAN ROTH Editor

1968—CARL YASTRZEMSKI

Carl Yastrzemski came to the majors in 1961, as Boston's successor to Hall of Famer Ted Williams in left field. Yaz's stellar outfield play, particularly handling caroms off Fenway Park's famous Green Monster in left field, soon silenced most of his critics. So did his hitting. He resurrected the Boston Red Sox franchise in 1967—their pennant-winning "Impossible Dream" season—winning the American League Triple Crown: batting .326, smacking 44 homers, and driving in 121 runs. That year, he also led in hits, runs, total bases, and won the Hickok Belt as the best professional athlete in the country—a monster season.

The race for the American League pennant in 1967 was one of the most exciting ever, coming down to Boston's final two games against the Minnesota Twins. To win the AL title, Boston needed to win both games. Yastrzemski drove in six runs and went 7 for 8 as Boston won both.

He was the American League's Most Valuable Player, *Sports Illustrated*'s Sportsman of the Year, an All-Star, and a Gold Glove winner. In 1966, the average attendance at Fenway Park, where the Red Sox finished in ninth place in a ten-team league, was 10,000. In 1967, it more than doubled to 21,000, and the Red Sox led the AL in home attendance with 1.7 million, more than double their 1966 total of 811,172.

Yastrzemski is the first player to have at least 100 hits in each of his first 20 seasons. He spent his entire 23-year career with the Red Sox. Yastrzemski retired with the most games played in a career and most for just one team—3,308. He is the first American League player with 3,000 (3,419) hits and 400 (452) home runs.

Yastrzemski batted .369 with three home runs and nine RBIs in the two losing World Series he played in, 1967 and 1975. He was an 18-time All Star who won seven Gold Gloves. His #8 was retired, he was inducted into the Hall of Fame, and in 2013 the Red Sox unveiled a statue of Yastrzemski at Fenway Park.

In and Around Baseball 1967:

August 18: Boston Red Sox slugger Tony Conigliaro is hit right below his left eye by a pitch from Jack Hamilton of the California Angels. Tony C recovers, but is never the same.

In the World Series, the St. Louis Cardinals' Bob Gibson puts out an incredible effort against the Red Sox. He won all three of his starts. All three were complete games, and one was a shutout. He struck out 26 in 27 innings and allowed only three runs as the Cardinals won 4–3. Gibson was the World Series MVP.

73¢

1969

54th EDITION
MAC

who's who
in BASEBALL

PETE ROSE

BOB GIBSON

DENNY McLAIN

Lifetime Records
Plus **PHOTOS**
of More Than
625 Players

CARL YASTRZEMSKI

PUBLISHED BY
Who's Who in Baseball Magazine Company, Inc.
ALLAN ROTH Editor

1969—DENNY MCLAIN, PETE ROSE, BOB GIBSON, CARL YASTRZEMSKI

Pitching for the Detroit Tigers, Denny McLain won 31 games in 1968—the most in a single season for an American Leaguer since 1931—and lost only six, for a winning percentage of .838, to lead the league. He's the last pitcher to win 30 games in a season.

An All-Star, he won the Cy Young Award and was the Most Valuable Player in the AL.

McLain was the son-in-law of Hall of Famer Lou Boudreau, making McLain the only man to join his father-in-law on the covers of *Who's Who in Baseball*.

McLain's Tigers won 103 games and the American League pennant.

Pete Rose was the National League Rooke of the Year in 1963 and spent the first 14 years of his career with his hometown Cincinnati Reds. Rose led the NL in hits in 1968, when he had 210, on his way to an all-time record 4,256. He also led the league with a .335 batting average.

Known as "Charlie Hustle" for his all-out, aggressive style of play, Rose was the NL's Most Valuable Player in 1973, and was among the top 10 in MVP voting in six seasons. He won two Gold Gloves, and was an All-Star 17 times, at first, second, and third as well as at left field and right field. In 1978, Rose had a 44-game hitting streak, the longest in the National League in the 20th century. Rose later managed the Reds, but accepted a lifetime suspension on April 24, 1989, for betting on games, a charge he denied for many years. He was ruled ineligible for Hall of Fame consideration.

Bob Gibson spent his entire 17-year major league career pitching for the St. Louis Cardinals. Gibson won it all in 1968: the National League Cy Young and Most Valuable Player Awards and a Gold Glove with a record of 22-9. He won 15 games in a row and led the NL with 268 strikeouts, 13 shutouts, and a league-leading microscopic 1.12 ERA. His Cardinals won the pennant.

Gibson was among the most intimidating pitchers in the game, although he never led the league in wild pitches or hit batters. After his playing days were over, he was the "attitude coach"—a unique position—for the Mets and the Braves. The Cardinals retired his uniform #45, and he was inducted into the Baseball Hall of Fame in 1981.

Carl Yastrzemski followed up his 1967 Triple Crown/MVP/pennant-winning season by leading the American League in 1968 with a .301 batting average—the lowest ever to lead the league. He also led in walks and on-base percentage, won another Gold Glove, and was again an All-Star as he was for 18 seasons. He was on base a league-leading 283 times.

Yastrzemski had the most putouts and most assists of all AL left fielders.

In and Around Baseball 1968:

Pitchers overwhelmed batters in 1968. The season became known as "The Year of the Pitcher." The average American League batting average was an abysmal .230, and Yaz was the only player to hit over .300 (.301) . . . Bob Gibson's ERA of 1.12 is the lowest in the 20th century; Don Drysdale pitched 58.2 consecutive scoreless innings; 339 shutouts were pitched in 1968; Gaylord Perry and Ray Washburn pitched no-hitters on consecutive days; the Mets and Astros played a scoreless game for 24 innings.

More hitting was needed, it was thought, to bring the fans to the stadiums. So Major League Baseball lowered the pitcher's mound from 15 inches to 10 inches and shrunk the strike zone . . . After 13 years in Kansas City, the Athletics become the second team (after the Braves) to move twice: this time, to Oakland, California . . . Pitching for the Athletics, Jim "Catfish" Hunter was only 22 when he went 3 for 4 at the plate with a double and 3 RBIs while pitching a perfect game on May 8, 1968, to beat the Minnesota Twins 4–0 . . . Willie Mays, who was the MVP of the All-Star Game in 1963, became the first man to win the award twice in 1968.

Opening Day, scheduled for April 8, was postponed until April 10, the day after the funeral of the Rev. Dr. Martin Luther King Jr . . . July 9: The first indoor All-Star Game is played at Houston's Astrodome . . . September 22: The Minnesota Twins try something different: Cesar Tovar plays all nine positions.

The Detroit Tigers beat the St. Louis Cardinals. Bob Gibson struck out a record 17 Tigers in Game 1, won two games, and even hit a home run for the Cards, but Mickey Lolich won three games as the Tigers prevailed 4–3.

75¢

55th EDITION

1970 *who's who*

in BASEBALL

HARMON KILLEBREW

WILLIE McCOVEY

DENNY McLAIN

MIKE CUELLAR

TOM SEAVER

Lifetime Records
○
Plus PHOTOS
of More Than
615 Players

PUBLISHED BY

Who's Who in Baseball Magazine Company, Inc.

ALLAN ROTH Editor

1970—TOM SEAVER, HARMON KILLEBREW, WILLIE MCCOVEY, DENNY MCLAIN, MIKE CUELLAR

1969 was the year of the "Miracle Mets," led by their ace pitcher, George Thomas Seaver. His nicknames said it all: "The Franchise" and "Tom Terrific." From 1962 to 1968, the New York Mets finished 10th, 10th, 10th, 10th, 9th, 10th, and 9th in the National League.

In 1967, Seaver was the Mets' first Rookie of the Year. Seaver led the National League with 25 wins and lost only seven games. He had five shutouts and an ERA of 2.21. In his third year in the majors, Seaver won the National League Cy Young Award, the Hickok Belt, *The Sporting News* National League Pitcher of the Year, and *Sports Illustrated*'s Sportsman of the Year. Seaver led the Mets to an improbable National League pennant, beating the Atlanta Braves, and won a game in the World Series. The Mets, the first expansion team to win a pennant, outdrew the crosstown New York Yankees by over a million! Seaver's #41 was the first number retired by the Mets.

Harmon "Killer" Killebrew, from Payette, Idaho, was the Washington Senators first "bonus baby" in 1954. He signed with the Senators before he turned 18 and spent 21 years with the Washington Senators/Minnesota Twins franchise. He played his final season in 1975 with the Kansas City Royals.

He hit at least 40 home runs seven times, and in 1969 hit a career-high 49 to lead the American League. He also walked 145 times and drove in 140 runs, both tops in the league. Killebrew was an All-Star and was the AL's Most Valuable Player.

Killebrew was a classic slugger: He hit 573 career home runs (putting him at #5 on the all-time list when he retired) and had over 100 strikeouts seven times. He played mostly first base, but he also played over 700 games at third and over 900 in the outfield. Killebrew was never ejected from a game.

Willie "Stretch" McCovey came by his nickname naturally. At 6'4", he was an inviting target at first base for the San Francisco Giants. Unlike the other Willie on the Giants, McCovey was a home-grown San Francisco Giant, not a New York transplant. In 1969, he smacked a career-high 45 home runs and drove in 126 RBIs, both tops in the National League. McCovey drew a league-leading *45* intentional walks.

An All-Star, he was voted the NL's Most Valuable Player and the MVP in the All-Star Game—a rare double. *The Sporting News* named McCovey their National League Player of the Year. But the Giants finished second in the NL's Western Division, won by the Atlanta Braves.

When the Giants moved to their new stadium, now known as AT&T Park, an inlet in San Francisco Bay's China Basin beyond the right field fence was dubbed "McCovey Cove." McCovey is one of the few big leaguers to play in four decades (1959–1980).

In 1969, Detroit Tigers pitcher Denny McLain led the American League with 24 wins and 325 innings pitched. He tied with Mike Cuellar of the Baltimore Orioles for the American League Cy Young Award, becoming the first American Leaguer to win in consecutive seasons. But the Tigers had a dreadful season, finishing 19 games behind the pennant-winning Baltimore Orioles.

Cuban-born Mike Cuellar was the mainstay of the Baltimore Orioles' pitching staff during their run to the 1969 American League pennant.

In 1969, he went 23-11 with a 2.38 ERA with a nasty screwball and a good curve. He and Denny McLain were the only co-winners of the Cy Young Award in history. Cuellar won 20 games four times.

Cuellar won Game 1 in the World Series against the upstart New York Mets—the only Oriole win.

In and Around Baseball 1969:

February 4: Bowie Kuhn, a lawyer for the National League, is elected as the fifth commissioner of baseball . . . The American League gets two new teams: the Kansas City Royals and the Seattle Pilots. The Pilots are bought by a Milwaukee used-car dealer named Alan "Bud" Selig, later the commissioner of baseball. In 1970, the Pilots become the Milwaukee Brewers . . . There are two new National League teams too: the Montreal Expos and the San Diego Padres . . . The first Major League Baseball game played outside the United States takes place as the Expos beat the St. Louis Cardinals at Montreal on April 14 . . . The 1969 All-Star Game ends in a tie when both teams run out of pitchers . . . September 22: Willie Mays of the San Francisco Giants hits his 600th career home run, just the second man to do so.

In their eighth year of existence, the Mets beat the Baltimore Orioles 4–1 in the World Series. 🏐

75¢   56th EDITION

1971 *who's who*
in BASEBALL

ALLAN ROTH Editor

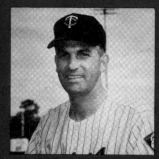
JIM PERRY

BOB GIBSON

BOOG POWELL

JOHN BENCH

Lifetime Records Plus **PHOTOS** of More Than 610 Players

PUBLISHED BY
Who's Who in Baseball Magazine Company, Inc.

1971—JOHNNY BENCH, JIM PERRY, BOB GIBSON, BOOG POWELL

The 1971 edition of *Who's Who in Baseball* was available in both red and blue.

Johnny Bench, considered by many the greatest catcher of all time, broke into the majors with the Cincinnati Reds in 1967 when he was 19. In 1968, he won a Gold Glove and was the first catcher to be the Rookie of the Year in the National League, and the first rookie catcher to be an All-Star. He was an All-Star for 14 of his 17 years in the majors, all with the Reds.

The 1970 season may have been his best. He led the National League with a career-best 45 home runs and 148 RBI—both records for catchers. He won his third of 10 consecutive Gold Gloves behind the plate and was the Most Valuable Player in the NL. Bench was named *The Sporting News* Major League Player of the Year. Bench powered the "Big Red Machine" to the 1970 National League pennant.

Bench had 389 career home runs, including 326 as a catcher, #1 on the all-time list when he retired. He's #3 today, behind only Mike Piazza and Carlton Fisk.

Bench revolutionized the art of catching with his one-handed technique and hinged mitt.

Jim Perry, a native of Williamston, North Carolina, pitched in the major leagues for 17 years. His younger brother Gaylord, also a pitcher, won 314 games and struck out 3,534 batters during his own 22-year career. In 1960, his second year in the majors, he led the American League with 18 wins for the Cleveland Indians. He later pitched for the Minnesota Twins, Oakland A's, and Detroit Tigers.

1970 was Perry's best year. He had a league-leading 40 starts—tied with three others—and 24 wins—tied with two others—although he also gave up the most home runs in the AL. Perry was in the top 10 in ERA, walks per nine innings, strikeouts, complete games, shutouts, and batters faced.

He was an All-Star and won the American League Cy Young Award. (When Gaylord won the Cy Young Award in 1972, they became the first brothers ever to win it.)

The Twins won the AL West title, but were swept 3-0 in the American League Championship Series.

Jim Perry retired after the 1975 season with 215 wins and 1,576 strikeouts.

Bob Gibson earned his second appearance on the cover of *Who's Who in Baseball* with his 23-7 record, most wins in the National League. He was an All-Star, won his second Cy Young Award, won over 30 percent of the Cardinals 76 wins in 1970, and won another Gold Glove for outstanding defense.

In 1970, John "Boog" Powell played first base for the Baltimore Orioles. He had a very good year, but led the American League in only one category: Most Valuable Player voting. Powell batted .297 with 35 home runs, 28 doubles, and 114 RBI. He earned a spot on the All-Star team. Powell was the first Oriole to hit three homers in one game.

Baltimore won the AL Eastern Division, the AL pennant, and beat the Cincinnati Reds 4–1 in the World Series.

When he appeared in the 1975 Cleveland Indians all-red road uniform—considered one of the ugliest of all time—the 6'4", 230-pound Powell, who always struggled with his weight, was said to resemble a giant blood clot.

In and Around Baseball 1970:

Willie McCovey of the San Francisco Giants hit at least one home run in every National League ballpark . . . April 22: After receiving his 1969 Cy Young Award at Shea Stadium, New York Mets pitcher Tom Seaver strikes out 19 San Diego Padres, including a record 10 in a row . . . May 10: Hoyt Wilhelm of the Atlanta Braves becomes the first man to pitch in 1,000 games . . . May 12: "Mr. Cub" Ernie Banks hits his 500th home run . . . May 17: The Atlanta Braves' Hank Aaron smacks his 3,000th hit . . . July 14: In the bottom of the 12th inning of the All-Star Game, two things arrive at home plate at the same time, after Jim Hickman singled: Pete Rose, running from second base, and the ball. Instead of sliding, Rose runs into AL catcher Ray Fosse, knocking him over, scoring the winning run, and permanently injuring Fosse . . . July 18: Willie Mays of the San Francisco Giants gets his 3,000th career hit . . . October 3: Umpires call a one-day strike on the first day of both League Championship Series. Minor league umpires substitute. The umpires seek recognition of their union and raises.

The 1970 World Series is the first played on artificial turf, at Cincinnati's Riverfront Stadium. Baltimore wins the Series 4–1. 🏐

$1.00

1972 who's who in BASEBALL

VIDA BLUE

JOE TORRE

Lifetime Records Plus PHOTOS of More Than 650 Players

ALLAN ROTH Editor

PUBLISHED BY
Who's Who in Baseball Magazine Company, Inc.

1972—JOE TORRE, VIDA BLUE

In 1972 there were two versions of the cover of *Who's Who in Baseball*: red and blue.

In 1971, the 11th year of his big-league career, Joe Torre had a career year for the St. Louis Cardinals. He hit .363 to lead the major leagues in batting—the first National League catcher to win the batting crown since Bubbles Hargrave in 1926. He also led both leagues with 230 hits and 137 RBI, hit 24 home runs, and had 352 total bases—also tops in the majors. Torre was voted the Most Valuable Player in the National League, and was named to the NL All-Star team (one of nine selections). But his Cardinals finished in second place, seven games behind the pennant-winning Pittsburgh Pirates.

Torre was inducted into the Baseball Hall of Fame in 2014, primarily because he won six American League pennants and four world championships between 1996 and 2003 as manager of the New York Yankees.

Joe Torre's brother Frank had been in the majors for four years before Joe debuted in 1960 with the Milwaukee Braves. Frank had a seven-year big-league career with the Braves and the Philadelphia Phillies. Frank's successful heart transplant as Joe managed the Yankees in the 1996 World Series riveted the attention of baseball fans all over the world. Before managing the Yankees, Torre had managed the Mets (where he had a losing record), Braves (barely winning record), and Cardinals (losing record). Torre was the first native New Yorker to manage the Yankees. He later managed the Los Angeles Dodgers for two years.

Vida Blue was 21 in 1971—his first full year in the majors. He won 24 games with a league-leading ERA of 1.82 and eight shutouts for the Oakland A's. He also led American League pitchers in fielding average. Blue won the American League Cy Young and Most Valuable Player Awards and was voted to the All-Star team. The A's lost to the Baltimore Orioles in the American League Championship Series.

Blue spent nine years with Oakland, whose owner once offered him a bonus to change his first name to "True," followed by six with the San Francisco Giants and two with the Kansas City Royals. He was the first pitcher to start an All-Star Game for both leagues. Blue and his wife were married on the pitcher's mound at the Giants' Candlestick Park.

In and Around Baseball 1971:

Batting helmets become mandatory in both leagues. Bob Montgomery, a backup catcher to the Red Sox Carlton Fisk, continued to play through 1979 with only a protective wafer in his hat . . . The Giants' Willie Mays opens the season by doing something nobody has done before: he homers in the first four games . . . April 27: Hank Aaron of the Atlanta Braves hits his 600th career home run . . . July 31: With the American League behind 3–0 in the bottom of the third, Reggie Jackson of the Oakland A's pinch-hits for AL pitcher Vida Blue. Jackson's one-out blast hit the light tower 540 feet away. The AL wins 6–4—their first win in eight years, and their last until 1983 . . . September 1: The Pittsburgh Pirates field the first all-minority lineup in history . . . September 30: the second Senators team, managed by Ted Williams, plays its final game in Washington, DC, before moving to Arlington to become the Texas Rangers. Rowdy fans jump onto the field in the top of the ninth inning at Robert F. Kennedy Memorial Stadium with Washington leading 7–5, impeding play. They dig up the pitcher's mound and literally steal some of the bases including home plate. A forfeit was declared, giving the Yankees a 9–0 win.

In the 1971 World Series, the Pittsburgh Pirates beat the Baltimore Orioles 4–3. Roberto Clemente hits .414 with two homers and four RBI. He was the Most Valuable Player in the Series. Game 4 of the 1971 Series, played in Pittsburgh on October 13, is the first World Series game ever played at night. ⚾

$1.00   58th EDITION

1973 who's who
in BASEBALL

DICK ALLEN
A.L. M.V.P.

STEVE CARLTON
N.L. CY YOUNG AWARD WINNER

Lifetime Records Plus PHOTOS of More Than 660 Players

PUBLISHED BY
Who's Who in Baseball Magazine Company, Inc.

1973—STEVE CARLTON, DICK ALLEN

Who's Who in Baseball was available in two colors—red and blue. And for the first time, *Who's Who in Baseball* notes MVP and Cy Young Awards on the cover.

Steve Carlton—"Lefty"—started his major league pitching career with the St. Louis Cardinals in 1965. Five teams and 24 years later, he had won 329 games and struck out 4,136 batters—#4 on the all-time list.

In 1972, with the Philadelphia Phillies, Carlton won the Triple Crown of Pitching, leading the National League with 27 wins—46 percent of his team's *total* wins—310 strikeouts, and a minuscule 1.97 ERA. He also had 30 complete games. Carlton won the Hickok Belt as the best pro athlete in the country. Carlton won his first of four Cy Young Awards and won the first of his four *Sporting News* NL Pitcher of the Year Awards. But the Phillies had a truly awful season: last place, 59-97, 37½ games behind the first place Pittsburgh Pirates.

Carlton led the NL in wins four times with six 20-win seasons. He was a workhorse, leading the NL in innings pitched five times (he's #9 on the all-time list) and three times in complete games. He faced the most batters in a season seven times. For five seasons he had the highest fielding average in the league: a perfect 1.0. He was a 10-time All-Star. Carlton was not a bad hitter either: he batted .201 with 13 career home runs.

Dick (or Richie) Allen, from Wampum, Pennsylvania, was the National League Rookie of the Year in 1964 with the Philadelphia Phillies. That year, he had 201 hits.

In 1972, playing mostly at third base with the Chicago White Sox, he led the American League with 37 homers, 99 walks, 70 extra base hits, and 113 RBIs. He was also #1 in on-base percentage and slugging percentage. Allen was among the league leaders in hits, doubles, triples, total bases, and runs scored. Allen was an All-Star and the AL's Most Valuable Player.

Allen spent 15 years in the majors with five teams and retired in 1978 with 351 career home runs and a batting average of .292.

In and Around Baseball 1972:

Major league baseball players went on strike from April 1 to April 13 . . . On May 13, the Milwaukee Brewers beat the Minnesota Twins 4–3 in 22 innings. The game started on May 12 but was suspended after 21 innings. The game, which had 30 hits and 39 runners left on base, took 5 hours and 47 minutes to complete . . . June 19: By a vote of 5–3, the US Supreme Court upholds baseball's antitrust exemption, ruling against outfielder Curt Flood . . . July 10: Johnny Bench appears on the cover of *Time* magazine . . . December 31: Pittsburgh Pirates star Roberto Clemente dies when his plane, overloaded with relief supplies, crashes into the ocean on its way from Puerto Rico to earthquake-ravaged Managua, Nicaragua. The five-year waiting period is waived, and Clemente, with exactly 3,000 hits, is enshrined as a member of the Baseball Hall of Fame in early 1973 . . . Gaylord Perry of the Cleveland Indians wins the Cy Young Award, joining his brother Jim, who won it in 1970 with the Twins, as the only brothers to win Cy Young Awards.

Because of the disruption in the season by the players' strike in April, the Detroit Tigers played one more game than the Boston Red Sox. On the next-to-last day of the season, Detroit beat Boston to win the AL East by ½ game.

The Oakland Athletics beat the Cincinnati Reds 4–3 in the World Series, the first world championship in the Bay Area. It is the Athletics' first Series victory since the Philadelphia A's won in 1930. 🄻

$1.00 59th EDITION

1974 who's who in BASEBALL

Lifetime Records Plus **PHOTOS** of More Than 660 Players

NOLAN RYAN
383 STRIKEOUTS

REGGIE JACKSON
A. L. M.V.P.

PETE ROSE
N. L. M.V.P.

PUBLISHED BY
Who's Who in Baseball Magazine Company, Inc.

1974—NOLAN RYAN, REGGIE JACKSON, PETE ROSE

Lynn Nolan Ryan—the "Ryan Express"—from Refugio, Texas, was drafted by the New York Mets in 1965—the 295th player chosen. After five losing seasons, the Mets traded him to the California Angels in 1971 as part of a five-player deal for Jim Fregosi—the worst trade in Mets history.

Ryan was one of the first big leaguers to use weight training as part of his conditioning regimen. His fastball was once clocked at 100.9 mph. Ryan wound up starting 773 games—more than any pitcher except Cy Young—winning 324, throwing a record seven no-hitters, striking out a record 5,714 batters—839 Ks more than #2, Randy Johnson—and pitching an incredible 27 seasons. Ryan had more strikeouts than innings pitched.

In 1972, Ryan struck out 329 batters—the first right-hander since Bob Feller in 1946 to whiff 300 batters in a season.

On September 27, 1973, facing the Minnesota Twins in his final start of the year for the Angels, Ryan struck out the final batter he faced—Rich Reese—setting the major league mark of 383 strikeouts in a season, beating Sandy Koufax's previous mark by one. Ryan also walked a league-leading 162. His record was 21-16 for the fourth-place Angels. Despite all his accomplishments—including being the first pitcher to strike out 2,000 batters in both leagues—one award eluded Ryan: He never won the Cy Young Award.

Whatever you were doing, you stopped to watch or listen when Reggie Jackson came up to bat. He was that explosive, that exciting. He even looked good striking out, which he did quite often, leading the American League in Ks five times. Thirty-eight years after he retired in 1987, he still holds the unenviable record for most strikeouts in a career—2,597.

But he looked better smashing home runs, which he did 563 times, 13th on the all-time list. In 1972, Jackson was one of the first players since 1936 to have a moustache. Jackson is also one of the most successful ballplayers who wore glasses.

In 1973, with the Oakland A's, he led the AL with 32 home runs and 99 runs scored. He hit .293 and was an All-Star and the AL Most Valuable Player. In 1980, his batting average was exactly .300.

Jackson, a 14-time All-Star, was at his best in the postseason, hence his nickname—"Mr. October." He hit .357 with 10 home runs in five World Series with the A's and the New York Yankees. Jackson also played in 11 League Championship Series. As a Yankee in the 1977 World Series, he homered in his final at-bat of Game 5. In Game 6, he hit three home runs off three different pitchers—giving him four consecutive home runs—to beat the Los Angeles Dodgers 4–2.

Pete Rose won his only Most Valuable Player award in 1973 and was tops with 680 at-bats, 230 hits, 181 singles, and a .338 batting average—his third batting title. The Reds won the National League West, but were defeated in the League Championship Series by the New York Mets.

In and Around Baseball 1973:

In an "experiment," the American League creates a new position—the "designated hitter," who bats (usually instead of the pitcher) but does not play the field . . . July 15: Unable to get anywhere with a bat against Nolan Ryan of the California Angels—he'd struck out twice already—the Detroit Tigers' Norm Cash comes to bat in the ninth inning wielding a piano leg. Reverting to a traditional bat, Cash pops out . . . July 15: Ron Blomberg of the New York Yankees becomes the first designated hitter. He walks . . . Tom Seaver becomes the first pitcher to win the Cy Young Award without winning 20 games. He wins only 19, but he leads the National League in ERA, strikeouts, and complete games . . . In the worst and most controversial trade in the history of sports, New York Yankee pitchers Mike Kekich and Fritz Peterson trade wives, families, even pets . . . Darrell Evans, Davey Johnson, and Hank Aaron of the Atlanta Braves become the first three teammates to hit at least 40 home runs in a season.

The Oakland Athletics win their second of three consecutive World Series, beating the New York Mets 4–3. Reggie Jackson wins the Series MVP with one homer, six RBIs and a .310 batting average. He was World Series MVP again in 1977—the first position player to be named World Series MVP twice.

$1.25

60th EDITION

1975 who's who in BASEBALL

Lifetime Records Plus PHOTOS of More Than 700 Players

JEFF BURROUGHS
A. L. M.V.P.

STEVE GARVEY
N. L. M.V.P.

LOU BROCK
118 STOLEN BASES

PUBLISHED BY
Who's Who in Baseball Magazine Company, Inc.

1975—LOU BROCK, JEFF BURROUGHS, STEVE GARVEY

Lou Brock, from El Dorado, Arkansas, went to Southern University on an academic scholarship. Brock broke into the majors in 1961 with the Cubs and played in Chicago for the first three years of his career. On June 15, 1964, he was involved in a six-player trade with the St. Louis Cardinals for Ernie Broglio and two others—one of the most lopsided major league trades of all time.

Brock blossomed with the Cardinals. He led the National League in stolen bases for eight seasons and retired with a career total of 938, surpassing 19th-century star "Sliding" Billy Hamilton's 914 and Ty Cobb's 897. Today, only Rickey Henderson has eclipsed Brock's career stolen base mark.

In 1964, Brock's first season in St. Louis, he hit .348. He hit over .300 eight times. In 1974, Brock stole 118 bases, breaking Maury Wills's previous single-season record of 104, which had stood since 1962. The record stood until it was broken by Rickey Henderson's 130 in 1982. After 41 years, 118 stolen bases is still the NL single-season record. Brock still holds the NL career stolen base record of 938. In 1974, Brock was an All-Star.

He retired with a .293 batting average and 3,023 hits. Brock was later ordained as a minister and was inducted into the Baseball Hall of Fame in 1985. His #20 was retired by the Cardinals. The National League's top base stealer is given the annual "Lou Brock Award."

In 1974, Jeff Burroughs of the Texas Rangers—the first pick of the 1969 amateur draft—hit 25 home runs and had 118 RBIs—33 more than in 1973, and the most in the American League. He turned five double plays as a right fielder—the most in the AL—and was third in total bases with 279. He raised his batting average by 22 points to .301, earning the 23-year-old an All-Star selection and the AL Most Valuable Player Award.

He was the first Texas Ranger to appear on the cover of *Who's Who in Baseball*. But Burroughs's fine season didn't help the Rangers—they finished in third place behind the AL West champion Oakland Athletics.

Steve Garvey's father Joe drove the Los Angeles Dodgers bus during spring training in the 1950s. His son grew up to be one of the pre-eminent first basemen of his era with the Dodgers and later the San Diego Padres. Garvey led the National League in putouts at first base six times. His fielding led the NL five times.

The Dodger star hit .312 in 1974 and won both a Gold Glove and the NL Most Valuable Player award. He had 21 home runs and exactly 200 hits—one of six seasons when he hit at least 200. He was an All-Star—as a write-in selection—for the first of 10 times and was named the MVP of the All-Star Game. Twenty-eight years after he retired in 1987, Garvey still holds the NL record for consecutive games played: 1,207.

In and Around Baseball 1974:

While Yankee Stadium is refurbished, the Yankees play all their home games in 1974 and 1975 at Shea Stadium, home of the Mets . . . April 4: Herb Washington, a world-class sprinter, makes his debut as the Oakland A's "designated runner." In his two-year career, he scores 33 runs with 31 stolen bases—0 at-bats, 0-hits . . . April 8: In his first at-bat of the Braves home opener in Atlanta, Hank Aaron hits career home run #715, breaking Babe Ruth's all-time record . . . July 19: Dick Bosman of the Cleveland Indians pitches a no-hitter against the Oakland Athletics. It would have been a perfect game but for Bosman's own error—a wild throw to first on a comebacker . . . September 25: Los Angeles Dodger southpaw Tommy John undergoes a new operation which rejuvenates his career, and eventually bears his name: Dr. Frank Jobe removes a tendon from John's right wrist and grafts it to his left elbow. John is back on the mound in 1976, pitches through age 46, and wins 170 more games. Hundreds of players, mostly pitchers, eventually undergo the procedure.

In the 1974 all-California World Series, the Los Angeles Dodgers faced the Oakland Athletics. Oakland won their third straight championship. Rollie Fingers was voted the Most Valuable Player in the Series, with four appearances, a 1-0 record with two saves, and six strikeouts in 9⅓ innings.

$1.25

61st EDITION

1976 who's who in BASEBALL

Lifetime Records Plus **PHOTOS** of More Than 700 Players

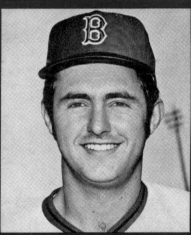

FRED LYNN — BOSTON
A.L. M.V.P.

JOE MORGAN — CINCINNATI
N.L. M.V.P.

"HAPPY BIRTHDAY"

NATIONAL LEAGUE 1876-1976

AMERICAN LEAGUE 1901-1976

PUBLISHED BY
Who's Who in Baseball Magazine Company, Inc.

1976—FRED LYNN, JOE MORGAN

The 1976 edition of *Who's Who in Baseball* was available in either red or blue.

Nobody ever had a rookie season like Fred Lynn did in 1975 for the Boston Red Sox. While others had earned Rookie of the Year honors, *nobody* before Lynn had been both Rookie of the Year *and* Most Valuable Player *in the same season*. Only Ichiro Suzuki in 2001 has won both in the same year since.

Lynn hit .419 with the Red Sox in 1974, but he played in only 15 games, so he still qualified as a rookie in 1975. That year, the 23-year-old Chicagoan hit .331 (second only to Rod Carew's .359) and led the majors with 47 doubles. He won a Gold Glove (one of four) for his play in center field and was selected to the All-Star team—the first of nine consecutive selections. He also led the American League in on-base percentage, slugging percentage, was second to Reggie Jackson with 75 extra base hits, third in RBIs, fourth in total bases, tied for fifth in triples, fifth in on-base percentage, and seventh in triples and hits (tied). He was on base 240 times.

After seven years with the Red Sox, Lynn moved on to the California Angels, Baltimore Orioles, Detroit Tigers, and San Diego Padres. He retired at 38 in 1990 with a .283 career batting average and 306 home runs.

Lynn's grand slam in 1983—on the 50th anniversary of the first All-Star Game—was the first in All-Star Game history.

Although Joe Morgan stood only 5'7" and weighed 160 pounds, the second baseman was a giant on the field. In 1975, Morgan was an integral part of Cincinnati's "Big Red Machine," which beat the Boston Red Sox 4–3 in a thrilling World Series, then won it again, sweeping the New York Yankees in 1976. In previous seasons, Morgan had led the National League in triples, runs scored, walks, on-base percentage, and fielding percentage.

In 1975, he hit .327, smacked 27 home runs, stole 67 bases, scored 107 runs, and led the NL with 132 walks and a .466 on-base percentage. He was selected to the All-Star team, won a Gold Glove (one of four), and was the first second baseman to win consecutive Most Valuable Player Awards—1975 and 1976. Morgan was *The Sporting News* Major League Player of the Year.

His career numbers are outstanding, including 268 home runs—#4 for second basemen—and 689 stolen bases, 11th on the all-time list. He was elected to the Cincinnati Reds Hall of Fame and the National Baseball Hall of Fame.

In and Around Baseball 1975:

Frank Robinson becomes the first black manager in baseball, as he is named to manage the Cleveland Indians . . . June 1: Nolan Ryan of the California Angels throws his record-tying fourth career no-hitter . . . December 23: It's a new era for baseball: arbitrator Peter Seitz voids baseball's "reserve clause" and declares Dave McNally and Andy Messersmith free agents . . . Tom Seaver of the New York Mets becomes the first right-hander to win three Cy Young Awards . . . The California Angels hit a total of 55 home runs all season.

The Red Sox won the AL pennant in 1975, their first since 1967. The 1975 World Series was an All-Red affair—the Reds against the Sox. The Reds—the Big Red Machine featuring such stars as Pete Rose, Tony Perez, Joe Morgan, Johnny Bench, Ken Griffey Sr., Cesar Geronimo, George Foster, Pedro Borbon Sr., and Don Gullett—prevailed 4–3. Rose hit .370 with 10 hits and two RBI. He was the Series MVP.

$1.50

1977

62nd EDITION

who's who

in BASEBALL

Lifetime Records
Plus PHOTOS
of More Than
700 Players

THURMAN MUNSON — NEW YORK
A.L. M.V.P.

JOE MORGAN — CINCINNATI
N.L. M.V.P.

PUBLISHED BY
Who's Who in Baseball Magazine Company, Inc.

1977—THURMAN MUNSON, JOE MORGAN

Thurman Munson was the American League's Rookie of the Year in 1970. In 1976, the New York catcher was the AL's Most Valuable Player—the first Yankee to be both. He led the Yankees to their first pennant since 1964 and their first of three in a row.

Munson had a very solid season—17 home runs, 105 RBI, a batting average of .302 and an All-Star selection, but his only league-leading statistic was passed balls (12). Although Munson hit .529 in the 1976 World Series, the Yankees were swept by the Cincinnati Reds' "Big Red Machine."

Munson was the heart and soul of the Yankees of the 1970s. At the start of the 1976 season, Munson was named team captain—the Yankees' first since Lou Gehrig. He was not a media darling; he thought his job was to hit and to catch. In order to spend more time with his family in Akron, Munson bought a Cessna Citation twin-engine jet. He was practicing takeoffs and landings in Akron when he died in a crash on August 2, 1979. His number 15 was retired, and his locker in the Yankee Stadium clubhouse remains untouched.

In 1976, Joe Morgan helped his Cincinnati Reds win the National League pennant by 10 games. He won his fourth Gold Glove at second base and was an All-Star for the second straight season, batting .320 with 27 home runs. Morgan led the NL with an on-base percentage of .444 and a slugging average of .576. His 60 stolen bases and 62 extra base hits were second in the league. He was named *The Sporting News* Major League Player of the Year and the National League MVP for the second consecutive season.

In and Around Baseball 1976:

April 17: Mike Schmidt of the Philadelphia Phillies connects for four homers against the Chicago Cubs. Schmidt is the first National Leaguer to hit four homers in consecutive at-bats . . . August 8: In the first game of a doubleheader against Kansas City, the Chicago White Sox try something new and dreadful: They beat the Royals 5–2 while wearing short pants. Owner Bill Veeck's idea does not catch on . . . In Game 5 of the ALCS, Chris Chambliss of the New York Yankees faces Mark Littell of the Kansas City Royals in the bottom of the ninth inning. With the game tied at 6, Chambliss hits one of the most famous walk-off home runs in history. Overjoyed Yankee fans swarm onto the field, preventing Chambliss from touching home plate. He later emerges from the dugout with a police escort to step on the plate . . . Jim Palmer of the AL Baltimore Orioles wins his second consecutive Cy Young Award.

The 1976 World Series pitted two of the best and most competitive catchers in the game against each other: Thurman Munson of the New York Yankees against Johnny Bench of the Cincinnati Reds. Munson hit .529 in the Series with nine hits. Bench hit .533 as he led the Reds in a sweep of the Yankees. Bench was voted the Series Most Valuable Player with two homers and six RBIs.

$1.50

63rd EDITION

1978 who's who in BASEBALL

Lifetime Records Plus **PHOTOS** of More Than 750 Players

GEORGE FOSTER—CINCINNATI
N.L.M.V.P.

ROD CAREW—MINNESOTA TWINS
A.L.M.V.P.

PUBLISHED BY
Who's Who in Baseball Magazine Company, Inc.

1978—GEORGE FOSTER, ROD CAREW

By 1972, George Foster had been a big part of the Cincinnati Reds' "Big Red Machine" for six years, but he really turned it on in 1977. He became the seventh player to hit at least 50 homers in a season when he hit 52 home runs (including a record 31 on the road)—the most in the National League since Ralph Kiner hit 54 in 1949. (Willie Mays had also hit 52 in 1965.) Foster and Mays's 52 would not be topped in the NL until Mark McGwire's 70 in 1998.

Foster, mostly a left fielder, also led the NL with 388 total bases, 85 extra base hits, 124 runs scored, 149 RBI, and a slugging average of .631. He was elected to the All-Star team and was chosen the NL's Most Valuable Player.

But the Los Angeles Dodgers won the NL West by 10 games.

Rod Carew was born on a moving train in the Panama Canal Zone. During his 19-year career with the Minnesota Twins and the California Angels, he won the American League batting crown seven times including four in a row, led the league in hits three times, stole home 17 times, and retired in 1985 with a career batting average of .328. In 1972, Carew performed a very rare feat: He won the AL batting crown, hitting .318, with 0 home runs.

1977 may have been the best year of his career. He led the AL with 16 triples, 239 hits, 171 singles, a .388 batting average, 15 intentional walks, an on-base percentage of .449, and for the only time, he led the AL in runs scored with 128. He also stole 23 bases.

The AL Rookie of the Year in 1967, and an All-Star for 18 of his 19 years, Carew was the AL's Most Valuable Player in 1977. He was also named *The Sporting News* Major League Player of the Year and won the Roberto Clemente Humanitarian Award. But his Twins finished in third place in the AL West, behind the champion Kansas City Royals.

Carew's #29 was retired by both the Twins and the Angels. He was inducted into the Baseball Hall of Fame in 1991.

In and Around Baseball 1977:

It's a new team in a new country for the American League—the Toronto Blue Jays debut . . . Bill James's self-published *Baseball Abstract* goes on sale. His statistical analysis of the game opens up a new era in baseball research.

In their first meeting since 1963, the New York Yankees beat the Los Angeles Dodgers 4–2 in the World Series.

$1.75

64th EDITION

1979 who's who in BASEBALL

Lifetime Records
Plus **PHOTOS**
of More Than
800 Players

JIM RICE
A.L. M.V.P.

DAVE PARKER
N.L. M.V.P.

Ron Guidry
A.L. Cy Young Award

PUBLISHED BY
Who's Who in Baseball Magazine Company, Inc.

1979—RON GUIDRY, JIM RICE, DAVE PARKER

After six years in the minor leagues, in 1978 the New York Yankees' Ron Guidry, nicknamed "Gator" and "Louisiana Lightning," won 25 games—the most in the majors—and lost just three—all to pitchers named Mike. With his nasty slider, he struck out 248 batters (37 years later, still the Yankee record), won his first 13 games in a row, and led the league with nine shutouts and a minuscule ERA of 1.74.

Guidry was an All-Star and won the Cy Young Award, but was beaten in Most Valuable Player voting by Jim Rice. He was *The Sporting News* Pitcher of the Year and Major League Player of the Year.

Guidry was the winning pitcher in the historic Yankees one-game playoff with the Boston Red Sox on October 2 to determine the American League East Champion, one of the best and most exciting games ever played—unless you're a Red Sox fan.

Guidry spent his entire 14-year major league career with the Yankees.

Jim Rice spent his entire 16-year career with the Boston Red Sox as a left fielder and designated hitter. In 1978, the Anderson, South Carolina, native had one of the best offensive seasons any batter ever had. He played in every game, and led the American League with 213 hits, 139 RBIs, 86 extra base hits, 46 home runs (the most by a Red Sox player since Jimmie Foxx's 50 in 1938), and 15 triples (a rare combination), with 406 total bases—the most since Joe DiMaggio's 418 in 1937 (only 20 players have ever had more) and a slugging percentage of .600. Rice was a bargain with a reported annual salary of $125,000.

Rice was the first player with three consecutive seasons (1977–1979) with 200 hits and 35 home runs. He was the most feared slugger of his day.

The Red Sox finished the season tied with their rivals, the New York Yankees, with 99 wins, and faced each other at Fenway Park, chosen by a coin flip for a historic one-game playoff to determine the winner in the AL East. The Yankees won on a home run by Bucky Dent and went on to the World Series.

6'5" Dave "Cobra" Parker won the Most Valuable Player award in the National League—the first Pittsburgh Pirate to win it since Roberto Clemente in 1966. Parker hit 30 homers for the Pirates and led the NL (for the second consecutive time) with a .334 batting average, and 340 total bases. Parker also had 12 triples and 32 doubles. His slugging percentage was .585, #1 in the NL, and he received a majors-leading 23 intentional walks. Parker also won a Gold Glove for his outstanding play in right field.

The Pirates finished the season 1½ games behind the champion Philadelphia Phillies in the NL East.

In and Around Baseball 1978:

Pete Rose of the Cincinnati Reds hits safely in 44 consecutive games, tying Willie Keeler's 81-year-old National League Record . . . June 30: Willie McCovey of the San Francisco Giants hits his 500th home run . . . August 25: Major league umpires go on strike for one day.

Guidry helped the Yankees to a 4–2 victory over the Los Angeles Dodgers in the World Series. He pitched a complete-game win in Game 3.

1980

who's who

65th EDITION

$1.95

in BASEBALL

Lifetime Records
Plus **PHOTOS**
of More Than
800 Players

WILLIE STARGELL
N.L.M.V.P. (co-winner)

KEITH HERNANDEZ
N.L.M.V.P. (co-winner)

DON BAYLOR
A.L.M.V.P.

PUBLISHED BY
Who's Who in Baseball Magazine Company, Inc.

1980—WILLIE STARGELL, KEITH HERNANDEZ, DON BAYLOR

Wilver "Willie" Stargell, born in Earlsboro, Oklahoma, spent his entire 21-year Hall of Fame career with the Pittsburgh Pirates. In previous seasons, he'd led the National League with 48 and 44 home runs, and once led with 43 doubles, 119 RBI, and 154 strikeouts.

But in 1979, at age 39, Stargell—affectionately called "Pops"—hit only 32 home runs, fifth best in the league, and batted only .281, not even in the league's top 10. Although Stargell didn't lead the National League in *any* major statistic, he and Keith Hernandez of the St. Louis Cardinals were the first co–Most Valuable Players in the NL.

Stargell, accompanied by Sister Sledge's song, "We Are Family," hit .455 in the Pirates' three-game sweep of the Cincinnati Reds in the League Championship Series (where he was MVP) and .400 with three home runs in Pittsburgh's 4–3 World Series victory over the Baltimore Orioles. Stargell was MVP there too.

Stargell hit 475 career home runs, more than any other Pirate. The Pirates retired Stargell's #8 in 1982. He was inducted into the Baseball Hall of Fame in 1988.

Keith Hernandez is widely considered one of the best-fielding first basemen in the game's history. He led the National League in putouts at first base for four seasons, including 1979, and in assists at first base five times. Six times (including 1979) he led NL first basemen in turning double plays. Hernandez won 11 straight Gold Gloves.

He played his first 10 years with the St. Louis Cardinals, then had seven good years with the New York Mets (he was named captain in 1987) before finishing his 17-year career with the Cleveland Indians in 1990. He went on to become a Mets broadcaster.

Although he was a five-time All-Star, and won 10 Gold Gloves at first base, he was the National League's co-MVP only once—in 1979, when he was tied with the Pirates' Willie Stargell. Hernandez led the NL by hitting .344, with 48 doubles and 116 RBIs. He was second in hits with 210. He was very selective at the plate, walking 80 times.

He played in two World Series and won both—with the Cardinals in 1982, and memorably with the Mets in 1986.

Don Baylor had a 19-year major league career. He was one of baseball's first free agents. In 1979, when he was a California Angel, he had his best season. He hit. 296 and played in every game, mostly as an outfielder and designated hitter. Baylor led both leagues with 139 RBIs and 120 runs scored, and hit 36 home runs—all career highs. He was an All-Star, and the American League's Most Valuable Player.

In 1985, he won the Roberto Clemente Humanitarian Award. Baylor hit 338 career home runs, stole 285 bases, and led the AL in being hit by a pitch for eight years. He holds the painful AL modern single-season record for being hit by a pitch with 35 and the career record with 267.

He was later a respected hitting coach and managed the Colorado Rockies to the NL West title in 1995. He also managed the Chicago Cubs.

In and Around Baseball 1979:

July 12: One of the most ill-conceived promotions ever: "Disco Demolition Night" at Chicago's Comiskey Park. Admission is 98¢, with a promise to blow up all disco records fans brought in between games of a doubleheader. Fans pour onto the field and render it unusable for the second game. The White Sox lose a 9–0 forfeit to the Detroit Tigers . . . Enos Cabell leads the Houston Astros with 9 home runs, as the team finishes with more triples (52) than home runs (49) for the entire season.

The Pittsburgh Pirates, led by Willie Stargell, beat the Baltimore Orioles 4–3 in the World Series.

1981

66th EDITION
$2.50

who's who
in BASEBALL

HANDY REFERENCE GUIDE TO BATTING & PITCHING STATISTICS

GEORGE BRETT
A.L.M.V.P.

OFFICIAL FACT SHEET FOR EVERY PLAYER

MIKE SCHMIDT
N.L.M.V.P.

1981—GEORGE BRETT, MIKE SCHMIDT

George Brett was the first Kansas City Royal to appear on the cover of *Who's Who in Baseball*. He was the Royals third baseman for 21 years. 1980 was the future Hall of Famer's best year. He hit 24 home runs and led both leagues with an astronomical .390 batting average—the highest in the league since Ted Williams's .406 in 1941. (In 1994, Tony Gwynn of the San Diego Padres hit .394, but that was a strike-shortened season.) Brett had 175 hits, an on-base percentage of .454, and a slugging percentage of .664.

Brett was the American League's Most Valuable Player, he won the Hutch Award, and he was named *The Sporting News* Player of the Year. The Royals won their first pennant, but lost the World Series 4–2 to the Philadelphia Phillies. Brett's brother Ken pitched in the majors for 14 years. George was inducted into the Baseball Hall of Fame in 1999.

Mike Schmidt played his entire 18-year Hall of Fame career as the slugging third baseman for the Philadelphia Phillies. He averaged 37 home runs per season, leading the National League in homers in eight years. Schmidt hit a total of 548 round-trippers.

In 1980, he hit 48 homers and drove in 121 runs—both tops in the NL and career highs. He won a Silver Slugger Award as the best-hitting third baseman in the league, was elected to the All-Star team, won a Gold Glove (one of 10), and was the Most Valuable Player in the National League, as he was again in 1981.

In and Around Baseball 1980:

Ben Oglivie, from Colon, Panama, becomes the first foreign-born home run champion. The Milwaukee Brewers outfielder hit 41 . . . Nolan Ryan signs with the Houston Astros, the first player to make $1 million per year. On July 4, he reaches career strikeout #3,000 . . . Pitchers for the Oakland Athletics have the most complete games in 34 years—94.

The Phillies won the National League pennant—their first since 1950—and met the Kansas City Royals in their first Fall Classic. In the ninth inning of Game 6, KC's Frank White hits a foul popup by the first base dugout. Phillies catcher Bob Boone grabs it, but drops the ball—right into Pete Rose's glove. Out! The Phillies won the Series 4–2.

1982

who's who

67TH EDITION
$2.95

in BASEBALL

LIFETIME RECORDS of More Than 750 Players Plus **PHOTOS**

HANDY REFERENCE GUIDE TO BATTING & PITCHING STATISTICS

ROLLIE FINGERS
A.L. MVP &
Cy Young Winner

OFFICIAL RECORDS OF EVERY PLAYER

FERNANDO VALENZUELA
N.L. Cy Young &
Rookie of the Year
Awards

1982—FERNANDO VALENZUELA, ROLLIE FINGERS

When Fernando Valenzuela pitched at home for the Los Angeles Dodgers in 1981, he added a breath of fresh air—and lots of filled seats—at Dodger Stadium. There was even a name for it: "Fernandomania." Valenzuela was the first Dodger pitcher on the cover of *Who's Who in Baseball* since Sandy Koufax in 1967.

He was a late-season call-up in 1980, and pitched only 17.2 innings in 10 games, with no starts and two victories. But in 1981, at the age of 20, the screwballer from Navojoa, Mexico—the youngest of 12 children—was packing the fans in. There was something very strange about his delivery: He took his eyes off the catcher's target and looked up in the sky. But there was nothing strange about his results.

His record was 13-7 for a team that won only 36 games in the strike-shortened season. Valenzuela led the National League with 11 complete games and eight shutouts. He won his first 10 games. He also led the NL with 180 strikeouts over 192.1 innings. He was the first rookie to win the National League Cy Young Award, was voted the Rookie of the Year, and was named both *The Sporting News* National League Pitcher of the Year and Major League Player of the Year.

Rollie Fingers was the first pitcher to record 300 saves. In 1972, he led the Oakland Athletics to their first World Series, which they won on his Game 7 save.

In 1981, he led the American League in saves for the third time, with 28—enough for a Cy Young Award and a Most Valuable Player Award.

In 1972, team owner Charles Finley—desperate for a cheap promotion—offered his players a bonus of $300 if they grew moustaches by Father's Day. Fingers' handlebar moustache became his trademark. Indeed, at the end of his career, he was going to sign with the Cincinnati Reds, but they required that he shave his moustache. Moustache intact, he retired instead in 1985.

In 1981, he won his fourth Rolaids Relief Man of the Year Award. Fingers also held the since-broken record for most World Series saves with seven.

Fingers appeared in 16 World Series games. He was inducted into the Baseball Hall of Fame in 1992.

In and Around Baseball 1981:

April 25: Because his team is having a tough time getting around on breaking balls (his words), Seattle Mariners manager Maury Wills orders the Kingdome grounds crew to enlarge the batter's box by one foot. He is suspended for two games . . . May 15: Indians pitcher Len Barker throws a perfect game to beat the Toronto Blue Jays in Cleveland before 7,290 fans . . . June 12–July 31: Players go on strike for 49 days, seeking free agency and more money. When the season ends, a unique playoff system is implemented: the winner of the first half against the winner of the second half.

The Los Angeles Dodgers beat the New York Yankees 4–2 in the World Series. Because of the strike, the Dodgers end up with the fewest wins of any world champion—63. 🔵

1983

68TH EDITION
$3.50

who's who

BASEBALL
in

LIFETIME RECORDS of More Than 800 Players Plus PHOTOS

HANDY REFERENCE GUIDE TO BATTING & PITCHING STATISTICS

NEW

RECORDS OF ALL 26 MAJOR LEAGUE MANAGERS

ROBIN YOUNT
A.L. Most Valuable Player

DALE MURPHY
N.L. Most Valuable Player

1983—ROBIN YOUNT, DALE MURPHY

Robin Yount earned his nickname "The Kid." He broke into the major leagues when he was 18 as a first-round draft pick with the Milwaukee Brewers (then in the American League) in 1974. Yount spent his entire 20-year career with the Brewers, first as a shortstop and then as a center fielder.

Yount hit over 30 doubles eight times. He led the AL in doubles twice and in triples twice. Yount had the most hits in the 1980s, retiring with a career total of 3,142.

In 1982 he hit. 331, second in the league to Willie Wilson's .332, with 29 homers, 114 RBIs, and a league-leading 210 hits. He tied Hal McRae with 46 doubles. Yount led with 367 total bases. He was also #1 with 489 assists at shortstop. Yount was an All-Star, won a Gold Glove and a Silver Slugger Award, and won the AL Most Valuable Player Award. (His second MVP, in 1989, was as a center fielder.) He was *The Sporting News* AL Player of the Year. His Brewers won the American League pennant—their first—and became the first player to have four hits in a World Series game twice, but the Brewers lost the Series 4–3 to the St. Louis Cardinals.

Yount was elected to the Hall of Fame in 1999.

Dale Murphy was a first-round draft pick of the Atlanta Braves in 1974. He spent 15 of his 18 years in the big leagues as an outfielder with the Braves.

In 1982, he played in every game (one of four consecutive times he did that), hit 36 homers—second to Dave Kingman's 37—and led the National League with 109 RBIs. An All-Star, Murphy won a Silver Slugger Award (one of four) and a Gold Glove (one of five). He was voted the National League's Most Valuable Player. He was the MVP in 1983 too.

His Braves won the National League West in 1982 but lost to the St. Louis Cardinals in the League Championship Series, Murphy's only post-season experience.

Murphy retired in 1993—his only season with the Colorado Rockies—with 398 career home runs. He played in 740 consecutive games between September 27, 1981 and July 9, 1986—the 13th longest streak in history.

In and Around Baseball 1982:

May 6: Pitching for the Seattle Mariners, 43-year-old Gaylord Perry wins his 300th game . . . August 4: Joel Youngblood gets a hit for the New York Mets in a game against the Cubs in Chicago (off future Hall of Famer Ferguson Jenkins). Immediately after his trade to the Montreal Expos, he flies to Philadelphia and singles against future Hall of Famer Steve Carlton of the Phillies—the only player to get hits off Hall of Fame pitchers for two teams in two cities on the same day . . . August 7: Red Sox infielder Dave Stapleton faces Chicago White Sox pitcher Rich Dotson at Fenway Park. A foul ball into the first base field boxes hits four-year-old Johnny Keane in the head, fracturing his skull. Before anybody else moves, Jim Rice leaps from the dugout into the stands, picks Keane up, and carries him into the clubhouse for medical attention. Keane recovered and threw out the first pitch on Opening Day, 1983. Rice got a save . . . Steve Sax is the fourth L.A. Dodger in a row to be named NL Rookie of the Year, following Rick Sutcliffe (1979), Steve Howe (1980), and Fernando Valenzuela (1981).

In the World Series, the St. Louis Cardinals beat the Milwaukee Brewers 4–3. It was the Brewers first (and so far only) appearance in the Fall Classic.

69TH EDITION

$3.95

1984 *who's who*
in BASEBALL

LIFETIME
RECORDS
Of More Than
800 Players
Plus
PHOTOS

HANDY
REFERENCE
GUIDE TO
BATTING &
PITCHING
STATISTICS

RON KITTLE
A.L. Rookie-
Of-The-Year

DARRYL
STRAWBERRY
N.L. Rookie-
Of-The-Year

CAL RIPKEN, JR.
A.L. M.V.P.

1984—CAL RIPKEN JR., RON KITTLE, DARRYL STRAWBERRY

Cal Ripken Jr. was the 48th pick in the second round of the 1978 amateur draft. He broke into the majors at 20 with the Baltimore Orioles, where he spent his entire 21-year career. In 1982, as a shortstop, he hit 28 home runs, 32 doubles, and was the American League's Rookie of the Year. After that, he just got better.

In 1983, he led the AL in many statistics, including games played (162), plate appearances (726), at-bats (663), extra base hits (76), runs scored (121), hits (211), and doubles (47). He was second in total bases (343), batted .318, and hit 27 home runs.

Being 6'4" was not an impediment to Ripken being an All-Star shortstop: For the first of seven times, Ripken led all AL shortstops in assists. He also led all AL shortstops in double plays turned (for the first of eight times). Ripken was chosen to his first of *19 consecutive* All-Star teams, won a Silver Slugger Award (one of eight), was selected as *The Sporting News* Major League Player of the Year, and won the first of his two AL Most Valuable Player Awards. He led the Orioles to the American League East crown, six games ahead of the Detroit Tigers.

Baltimore beat the Chicago White Sox in the League Championship Series, then beat the Philadelphia Phillies 4–1 in the World Series, the Orioles' first championship since 1970.

Starting on May 30, 1982, Ripken played in every Orioles game (usually in every inning) for 14 consecutive seasons. During his streak, 3,713 major leaguers spent time on the disabled list. Ripken's streak ended on September 19, 1998 when he voluntarily benched himself. His record 2,632 consecutive games played eclipsed Lou Gehrig's 59-year-old record of 2,130—which had been considered unbreakable.

In 1989, he hit at least 20 home runs for the eighth straight year—breaking Ernie Banks's 27-year-old record (Ripken's record is 10). Ripken was the first man to start four consecutive All-Star Games at shortstop (1983–1987).

Ripken retired after the 2001 season with 3,184 hits, a career .276 batting average, and 431 home runs.

Between 1982 and 1991, Ron Kittle played 353 of his 843 career games as a designated hitter for the Chicago White Sox, New York Yankees, Cleveland Indians, and Baltimore Orioles.

In 1983, his first full year in the majors, Kittle hit only .254 but he drove in 100 runs and hit 35 home runs for the White Sox, third behind Jim Rice's 39. He homered once every 14.9 at-bats, highest in the American League. He was ninth in slugging, but led the AL with 150 strikeouts. Nevertheless, he was an All-Star and the AL's Rookie of the Year.

6'6" Darryl Strawberry, from Los Angeles's Crenshaw High School, was the New York Mets' first pick overall in the 1980 amateur draft. He worked his way up through the Mets minor league system, and after only 16 games at AAA, he broke into the major leagues on May 6, 1983. That year he hit 15 doubles, seven triples, and 26 home runs. He was the National League's Rookie of the Year. But that didn't help the Mets, who finished last in the AL East, with a 68-94 record, 22 games out of first place.

Strawberry was just getting started. In a 17-year career that saw him wear the uniforms of all four past and present New York teams—Mets, Yankees, Los Angeles Dodgers and San Francisco Giants—Strawberry was an eight-time All-Star; a two-time Silver Slugger winner; and the 1988 NL home run champ with 39, on his way to 335 career home runs. After his playing career and a string of criminal convictions, Strawberry became a minister.

In and Around Baseball 1983:

April 27: Nolan Ryan of the Houston Astros strikes out Brad Mills of the Montreal Expos to break Walter Johnson's career record of 3,509 strikeouts . . . July 4: Dave Righetti of the New York Yankees pitches a no-hitter . . . Reggie Jackson of the California Angels strikes out for his 2,000th time . . . The Seattle Mariners become the first team to play an entire season without a doubleheader.

The Baltimore Orioles beat the Philadelphia Phillies 4–1 in the 1983 World Series. It's the Orioles' first world championship since 1970. ⚾

70TH EDITION

$3.95

1985 *who's who in* BASEBALL

LIFETIME RECORDS
Of More Than 800 Players
Plus PHOTOS

HANDY
REFERENCE
GUIDE TO
BATTING &
PITCHING
STATISTICS

**WILLIE HERNANDEZ
A.L. M.V.P. &
Cy Young Winner**

**RYNE SANDBERG
N.L. M.V.P.**

0 71486 02736

5 5

1985—RYNE SANDBERG, WILLIE HERNANDEZ

After 13 games with the Philadelphia Phillies, Ryne Sandberg—named for pitcher Ryne Duren—was traded in 1981 to the Chicago Cubs, where he played for 15 years.

He had an outstanding year in 1984 at second base: 19 home runs, 36 doubles, a league-leading 19 triples, and 114 runs scored. He was second with 74 extra base hits, and third in slugging percentage. He was an All-Star (one of 10 consecutive selections), won the second of his eight Gold Gloves, a Silver Slugger Award, and was the National League's Most Valuable Player.

Led by Sandberg's bat and glove, the Cubs won the NL East, their first postseason appearance since 1945. They won it again in 1989, but lost both times in the National League Championship Series.

Sandberg stole 344 bases, had five seasons with over 25 home runs, and finished his career with 282. In 1990, he hit 40 home runs, the most by a second baseman since Dave Johnson in 1973.

Sandberg retired after a dismal 1994 season in which he batted only .238, but returned in 1996 for two more seasons. He hit over .300 five times and retired for good with a career batting average of .285.

He was elected to the Baseball Hall of Fame in 2005.

Guillermo Villanueva "Willie" Hernandez was a major league relief pitcher for 13 seasons. His first year with the Detroit Tigers in 1984 was his best season.

His won-lost record was an unspectacular 9-3, but he had 32 saves in a league-leading 80 games with an ERA of 1.92.

Hernandez was an All-Star and was named *The Sporting News* American League Pitcher of the Year. He also won the AL Cy Young and Most Valuable Player Awards.

Hernandez, a native of Puerto Rico, pitched in three games in the Fall Classic as the Tigers beat the San Diego Padres 4–1, their fourth world championship, and their first since 1968.

In and Around Baseball 1984:

March 3: Former college water polo player Peter G. Uebberoth is unanimously elected baseball's sixth commissioner . . . April 13: Pete Rose of the Montreal Expos gets his 4,000th career hit . . . September 17: Reggie Jackson of the California Angels hits career home run #500 . . . September 30: On the last day of the season for a California Angels club headed for an 81-81 second place finish in the AL West, Mike Witt throws a perfect game before 8,375 fans at Arlington Stadium to beat the Texas Rangers 1–0.

71st Edition

$3.95

1986 *who's who*
in **BASEBALL**

LIFETIME RECORDS
Of More Than 800 Players
Plus Photos

DWIGHT GOODEN
N.L. Cy Young
Winner

Don Mattingly
A.L. M.V.P.

Willie McGee
N.L. M.V.P.

HANDY REFERENCE GUIDE TO BATTING & PITCHING STATISTICS

1986—DWIGHT GOODEN, DON MATTINGLY, WILLIE MCGEE

A first-round draft pick by the New York Mets in 1982, Dwight Gooden was pitching in the majors by 1984, when he went 17-9 with a National League–leading 276 strikeouts. (Hence his nicknames, "Dr. K" and "Doc.") His ERA was 2.60. Gooden was the National League Rookie of the Year, and, at 17, the youngest All-Star ever.

In 1985, he pitched 16 complete games and won the NL Cy Young Award and as a Met, leading the National League with 24 wins, 268 strikeouts, and an ERA of 1.53, becoming the first to win the NL Triple Crown of Pitching since Steve Carlton in 1972. The Mets finished in second place in the NL East.

Don Mattingly—"Donnie Baseball"—had a storied 14-year career, all at first base with the New York Yankees. He played from 1982 to 1995.

Mattingly did not lead the league in batting in 1985, but he did hit .324—one of seven seasons in which he hit over .300. He led the American League with 48 doubles, 86 extra base hits, 145 RBI, and total bases (370—48 more than runner-up George Brett). He scored 107 runs. He was an All-Star (one of six selections), won a Gold Glove (one of nine), a Silver Slugger Award, and was the AL's Most Valuable Player. On March 1, 1991, Mattingly was named captain of the Yankees.

His only postseason experience was in the American League Division Series in 1995, which the Yankees lost to the Seattle Mariners 3–2. Mattingly hit .417 in the series.

The Yankees retired Mattingly's #23, and erected a plaque to him in Yankee Stadium's Monument Park. Mattingly later became a hitting coach and managed the Los Angeles Dodgers.

Willie McGee made his big-league debut with the St. Louis Cardinals in 1982 as a 23-year-old.

In 1985, the pencil-thin (6'1", 175 pounds) McGee led the National League with 216 hits—162 of them singles—18 triples, and a batting average of .353—.33 points ahead of the runner-up Pedro Guerrero, and at the time, tied with Mickey Mantle for the highest ever for a switch hitter. McGee was third in stolen bases with 56, but Vince Coleman literally ran away with the stolen base title with 110.

McGee was an All-Star, a Gold Glove and Silver Slugger winner, and was the NL's Most Valuable Player. The Cardinals won 101 games and won the NL East by three games. They also won the NL pennant, but lost 4–3 to the Kansas City Royals in an all-Missouri World Series.

In and Around Baseball 1985:

July 11: Nolan Ryan, pitching for the Houston Astros, strikes out the New York Mets' Danny Heep—Ryan's 4,000th strikeout . . . August 4: Tom Seaver of the Chicago White Sox gets career win #300, beating the New York Yankees. On the same day, Rod Carew of the California Angels gets his 3,000th hit . . . August 19: Pete Rose appears on the cover of *Time* magazine. On July 10, 1989, he became the second player to appear on the cover twice. Joe DiMaggio was the first . . . September 11: At home in Cincinnati, the Reds' Pete Rose gets hit #4,192—the most ever . . . October 6, the last day of the season: 46-year-old Phil Niekro blanks the Toronto Blue Jays for his 300th career win.

The all-Missouri 1985 World Series matched the St. Louis Cardinals against the Kansas City Royals in the "I-70 Series," named for the interstate highway that connects the two cities. This was the first World Series in which, to boost television ratings, all games were night games. Kansas City won 4–3—their first world championship.

1987 who's who in BASEBALL

72nd EDITION
$3.95
02736

LIFETIME RECORDS Of More Than 700 Players *Plus Photos*

HANDY REFERENCE GUIDE TO BATTING & PITCHING STATS

ROGER CLEMENS A.L. M.V.P. & Cy Young Winner

MIKE SCHMIDT N.L. M.V.P.

1987—ROGER CLEMENS, MIKE SCHMIDT

Picked by the Boston Red Sox as the 19th selection in the 1983 draft, Roger "The Rocket" Clemens made his debut on May 15, 1984. From the mid-1980s through the end of his career in 2007, when you thought "strikeouts," you thought Roger Clemens.

In 1986, he led the American League with 24 wins (with only four losses), and led the majors with an ERA of 2.48. He struck out 238, second only to Mark Langston's 245.

He was an All-Star (the first of 11 selections), the Most Valuable Player in the American League—just the ninth pitcher to be so named—and won the first of his record seven Cy Young Awards. Clemens was also the Most Valuable Player in the 1986 All-Star Game and *The Sporting News* AL Pitcher of the Year.

On April 29, 1986, before a crowd of barely over 13,000 at Fenway Park in Boston, in his fourth start after right-shoulder surgery, the 23-year-old Clemens struck out a record 20 Seattle Mariners. The previous 20th-century record was 19, shared by Tom Seaver, Nolan Ryan, and Steve Carlton. Clemens struck out 20 again on September 18, 1996.

Clemens led the Red Sox to the World Series in 1986, which they lost 4–3 to the New York Mets.

He led the American League in strikeouts five times and broke Walter Johnson's 88-year-old record for most strikeouts in AL history. Johnson's record of 3,509 had stood for 88 years since he retired in 1927. Clemens retired with 4,167 AL strikeouts. He also pitched for the Houston Astros in the National League for three years, where he struck out 505 batters.

His total of 4,672 career strikeouts puts him third on the all-time list, behind only Nolan Ryan and Randy Johnson.

Clemens won the Triple Crown of Pitching in 1997 and 1998 with the Toronto Blue Jays, one of only four pitchers to do so in consecutive years.

The others are Lefty Grove, Grover Alexander, and Sandy Koufax.

Clemens was later beset by legal problems related to his alleged use of performance-enhancing drugs.

Mike Schmidt hit .290 with 29 doubles, scored 97, drove in 119, and led the NL with 37 home runs for the 1986 Philadelphia Phillies. Schmidt earned his 10th trip to the All-Star Game, his 10th Gold Glove at third base, his sixth Silver Slugger Award, and was named the Most Valuable Player in the National League for the third time. But his Phillies had a disappointing season, finishing in second place in the NL East, 21½ games behind the Mets, who went on to win the World Series.

In and Around Baseball 1986:

April 7: Dwight Gooden of the New York Mets appears on the cover of *Time* magazine . . . April 7, Opening Day: Dwight Evans of the Boston Red Sox hits the first pitch of the season for a home run . . . In the fourth and fifth innings of the All-Star Game, the Los Angeles Dodgers' Fernando Valenzuela ties Carl Hubbell's 52-year-old record by striking out five American Leaguers in a row . . . July 6: Bob Horner, who never spent a day in the minors, hits four home runs for the Atlanta Braves in a game against the Montreal Expos . . . October 4: Greg Gagne of the Minnesota Twins hits two inside-the-park home runs . . . October 12: In Game 5 of the ALCS, with two strikes on him in the top of the ninth inning, Dave Henderson of the Boston Red Sox homers off Donnie Moore of the Anaheim Angels, to give Boston a 6–5 lead. The Angels tie the game in the bottom of the inning, but Boston wins in the 11th and wins the series 4–3.

The Red Sox, just one pitch away from winning their first World Series since 1918, lose Game 6 to the New York Mets, then lose Game 7 and the Series. 🌕

73rd Edition
$4.50
CC 02736

1988 *who's who* *in* BASEBALL

LIFETIME RECORDS
Of More Than 800 Players, *Plus Photos*

HANDY REFERENCE GUIDE TO BATTING & PITCHING STATS

ANDRE DAWSON
N.L. M.V.P.

GEORGE BELL
A.L. M.V.P.

MARK McGWIRE
A.L. Rookie of the Year

1988—MARK MCGWIRE, GEORGE BELL, ANDRE DAWSON

If ever a player could be said to have burst on the scene, it might be 6'5", 215-pound Mark McGwire—"Big Mac."

In 1987, the Oakland first baseman shattered the previous record for home runs by a rookie—38—by hitting an incredible 49. The old American League mark was 37, set by Al Rosen of the Cleveland Indians in 1950. McGwire might have hit even more home runs, but he missed a few games at the end of the season to be with his wife for the birth of their first child. McGwire also led the American League with a slugging percentage of .618 and was second in total bases with 344.

McGwire was an All-Star (the first of 12 selections) and the unanimous choice for American League Rookie of the Year. But Oakland finished third in the AL West.

McGwire hit over 40 home runs in six seasons. In 1998, he broke Roger Maris's 37-year-old record of 61 home runs by hitting 70. Over his 16-year career, he won a Gold Glove at first base, three Silver Slugger Awards, and hit 583 home runs—number 10 on the all-time list. The end of his career was marked by controversy over his alleged use of performance-enhancing drugs.

George Bell, an outfielder from San Pedro de Macoris in the Dominican Republic, was the first Toronto Blue Jay to appear on the cover of *Who's Who in Baseball*.

In 1987, Bell hit .308 with 32 doubles and 47 home runs (two behind #1 Mark McGwire), and led the American League with 83 extra base hits, 134 RBIs, and 369 total bases.

Although Bell led the American League in errors by a left fielder five times, in 1987 he led the AL with 15 assists by a left fielder.

He was an All-Star (the first of three selections), won a Silver Slugger Award, and was the Most Valuable Player in the American League. Bell was also *The Sporting News* Major League Player of the Year. His Blue Jays finished the season two games behind the division-winning Detroit Tigers.

Andre Dawson—"The Hawk"—was the National League Rookie of the Year in 1977 as a Montreal Expo. In 1987, he signed with the Chicago Cubs as a free agent, and things took off. Playing on grass after 11 years on Olympic Stadium's artificial turf in Montreal, Dawson led the National League with a career-high 49 home runs—the most in the NL since Willie Mays's 51 in 1955—137 RBIs, and 353 total bases. He was an All-Star, won a Gold Glove for his outfield play, and a Silver Slugger Award. The Cubs finished the season 18½ games out of first place, but Dawson was chosen the NL Most Valuable Player—the first MVP on a last place team.

Dawson retired after the 1996 season with 1,591 RBI, 2,774 hits, and 438 home runs. He was inducted into the Baseball Hall of Fame in 2010.

In and Around Baseball 1987:

Cal Ripken Sr. of the Baltimore Orioles becomes the first man to manage two sons—Billy and Cal Jr.—at the same time . . . For the first time, a World Series game is played indoors as the Minnesota Twins host the St. Louis Cardinals for Game 1 at the Hubert H. Humphrey Metrodome . . . Roger Clemens of the Boston Red Sox becomes just the fourth pitcher to win back-to-back Cy Young Awards . . . Nolan Ryan becomes the first pitcher to lead his league in ERA and strikeouts and not win the Cy Young Award. He was 18-6 with a dreadful Houston Astros team.

The Minnesota Twins beat the St. Louis Cardinals 4–3 to win their first World Series. 🌑

1989

who's who

74th Edition
$4.95

in BASEBALL

LIFETIME RECORDS
Of More Than
875 PLAYERS

plus PHOTOS!

KIRK GIBSON
N.L. M.V.P.

HANDY REFERENCE GUIDE TO BATTING AND PITCHING STATS

JOSE CANSECO
A.L. M.V.P.

1989—JOSÉ CANSECO, KIRK GIBSON

If you called central casting and said "Send me a baseball player," you'd probably get somebody built like 6'4", 240-pound José Canseco. His identical twin brother Ozzie had a brief major league career. The Canseco brothers hit 462 home runs—the most home runs ever by twins: 462 by José and 0 by Ozzie.

He'd been the American League Rookie of the Year with the Oakland Athletics in 1986, but by 1988 he'd turned it on, assisted, he later admitted, by using steroids. Canseco led both leagues with 42 home runs, 124 RBI, 76 extra base hits, and a .569 slugging percentage.

Canseco also stole 40 bases, becoming the American League's first 40-40 player—40 homers and 40 stolen bases. He was an All-Star, a Silver Slugger Award winner, and was chosen the AL Most Valuable Player.

After being a football star at Michigan State University, Kirk Gibson was a first-round draft pick by the Detroit Tigers in 1978. He spent parts of two seasons in the high minor leagues, then made his debut with the Tigers in late 1979.

In 1988, he was signed by the Los Angeles Dodgers as a free agent. Gibson hit .290 with 25 home runs and 76 RBI. Although Gibson was never an All-Star, he became the Most Valuable Player in his first year in the National League.

He led the National League in two statistics: most putouts in left field (314) and most errors in the outfield (12).

In and Around Baseball 1988:

September 8: A. Bartlett Giamatti, president of the National League, former president of Yale, with a PhD in Comparative Literature, is elected the seventh commissioner of baseball.

It's another all-California World Series in 1988, as the Los Angeles Dodgers beat the Oakland A's 4–1. 🏐

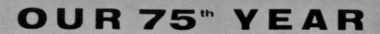

OUR 75th YEAR

1990 *who's who in BASEBALL*

75th Edition
$4.95

LIFETIME RECORDS
Of More Than
875 PLAYERS

plus
PHOTOS!

Kevin Mitchell
N.L. M.V.P.

HANDY REFERENCE GUIDE TO BATTING AND PITCHING STATS

Robin Yount
A.L. M.V.P.

1990—ROBIN YOUNT, KEVIN MITCHELL

Robin Yount made his second appearance on the cover of *Who's Who in Baseball* because of his stellar 1989. That year the former shortstop played mostly center field with a handful of games as the Milwaukee Brewers' designated hitter.

He won a Silver Slugger Award and was voted the American League's Most Valuable Player. Yount had 195 hits including 21 home runs. He drove in 103 and scored 101 runs, but didn't lead the league in any major statistic. Yount was second in the league in total bases (314); fourth in hits (195), and extra base hits (68); third in slugging percentage (.511); tied for third in runs scored (101); and fourth in batting (.318) and hits (195). The Brewers finished fourth in the AL East.

Yount had the most hits in the 1980s, and finished his career with 3,142 hits.

Giants left fielder Kevin Mitchell had the most home runs (47), RBIs (125), extra base hits (87), and total bases (345) in the majors in 1989. He was also second in putouts (293) from left field. Mitchell was *The Sporting News* Player of the Year, and the Most Valuable Player in the National League.

In and Around Baseball 1989:

June 5: Skydome—not "*The* Skydome," please—the new home of the Toronto Blue Jays, opens. It's the first stadium with a retractable roof . . . August 24: Pete Rose, baseball's all-time hits leader, agrees to a lifetime ban from baseball for gambling on the Cincinnati Reds, the team he managed . . . August 22: The Texas Rangers' Nolan Ryan makes the Oakland A's Rickey Henderson his 5,000th strikeout victim . . . September 1: Baseball Commissioner A. Bartlett Giamatti dies of a heart attack. His first deputy, Francis T. "Fay" Vincent Jr., succeeds him as commissioner.

The Earthquake World Series: At 5:04 p.m. Pacific Time on October 17, 1989, what became known as the Loma Prieta Earthquake struck the San Francisco Bay Area just before the start of Game 3 of the World Series between the Oakland Athletics and the Giants at San Francisco's Candlestick Park. It was the most powerful earthquake along the San Andreas Fault since the San Francisco Earthquake of 1906. While 57 people died in the earthquake, nobody was injured at the stadium. The game was postponed for 10 days. The A's eventually swept the Giants to win their fourth world championship.

OUR 76th YEAR

1991 *who's who*

76th Edition
$4.95

in BASEBALL

23

CECIL FIELDER
50 HOME RUN CLUB

NOLAN RYAN
5,308 STRIKEOUTS

LIFETIME RECORDS
Of More Than
910 PLAYERS

plus
PHOTOS!

HANDY
REFERENCE
GUIDE TO
BATTING AND
PITCHING
STATS

RYNE SANDBERG
NL HOME RUN CHAMP

1991—RYNE SANDBERG, CECIL FIELDER, NOLAN RYAN

Ryne Sandberg made his second appearance on the cover of *Who's Who in Baseball* in 1991 because he led the National League with 116 runs scored and 344 total bases—both personal bests. Sandberg was the first second baseman to hit at least 30 homers in consecutive years: 30 in 1989 and 40 in 1990.

He was second in the league with 73 extra base hits. Sandberg's 469 assists and 81 double plays at second base earned him his eighth Gold Glove, his seventh All-Star spot, and his fifth Silver Slugger Award.

It didn't make much difference, as his Cubs finished in fourth place in the NL East, 18 games behind the division-winning Pittsburgh Pirates.

Although Cecil "Big Daddy" Fielder struck out a league-leading 182 times in 1990, the hulking (6'3", 230 pounds) Detroit Tigers first baseman had a very good year when he made contact with his bat: 132 RBIs, 339 total bases, and a .592 slugging percentage. He smacked 51 home runs to lead the American League, and also led with one home run every 11.2 at-bats. Fielder also led the AL with 77 extra base hits and was second in runs scored with 104. Somehow Fielder managed one triple. He was voted to the All-Star team and won a Silver Slugger Award. But the Tigers finished in third place in the AL East, nine games behind the AL East champion Boston Red Sox.

In 2007, his son Prince hit 50 home runs for the Milwaukee Brewers, making Cecil and Prince Fielder the first father-and-son pair to hit 50 home runs each in a single season.

Defying science, logic, and age, Nolan Ryan got better as he got older. In 1990, after 24 years in the majors, the 43-year-old Ryan had 13 wins and 9 losses with a league-leading 232 strikeouts for the Texas Rangers.

He pitched his sixth no-hitter against the Oakland Athletics on June 11. He pitched a seventh no-hitter the next season when he was 44. Ryan has held the record for most strikeouts in a career—5,714—since he retired in 1993.

In and Around Baseball 1990:

The baseball season starts a week late because the players are locked out by the owners in a contract dispute. Missed games are later made up . . . April 11: Angels pitchers Mark Langston and Mike Witt pitch a combined no-hitter against the Seattle Mariners . . . June 29: Fernando Valenzuela of the Los Angeles Dodgers no-hits the St. Louis Cardinals. On the same day, Dave Stewart of the Oakland Athletics throws a no-hitter against the Toronto Blue Jays—the only time two no-hitters were thrown on the same day . . . July 18: At Boston's Fenway Park, Minnesota Twins third baseman Gary Gaetti does something nobody has ever done before: He starts two triple plays in the same game, which his team eventually loses . . . July 31: Nolan Ryan wins his 300th game . . . August 15: Terry Mulholland of the Philadelphia Phillies pitches what would have been a perfect game against the San Francisco Giants, but for an error by third baseman Charlie Hayes . . . September 14: For the first time in history, a father and son homer in the same game—in the same *inning*. In the first inning, Seattle Mariners Ken Griffey Sr. and Jr. both hit home runs off Kirk McCaskill of the California Angels.

The Cincinnati Reds, in first place in the NL West every day of the season, swept the Oakland A's in the World Series.

77th Edition
$4.95

1992 who's who in BASEBALL

LIFETIME RECORDS Of More Than 900 PLAYERS

Plus PHOTOS!

TERRY PENDLETON
NL MVP

CAL RIPKEN Jr.
AL MVP

ROGER CLEMENS
AL CY YOUNG WINNER

HANDY REFERENCE GUIDE TO BATTING AND PITCHING STATS

1992—ROGER CLEMENS, TERRY PENDLETON, CAL RIPKEN JR.

Boston's Roger Clemens led the American League with a 2.62 ERA, four shutouts, 271.1 innings pitched, and 241 strikeouts, but he had only 18 wins in 1991—Bill Gullickson and Scott Erickson were tied at 20—so he didn't win the Triple Crown of Pitching. But he did win his third Cy Young Award.

The Red Sox finished second as the Toronto Blue Jays won the American League East.

After seven years with the St. Louis Cardinals, third baseman Terry Pendleton signed with the Atlanta Braves as a free agent in 1990. The change of scenery did wonders for his performance. In 1991 Pendleton led the National League with a .319 batting average, 187 hits, and 303 total bases. He had 22 home runs and 105 RBIs—a career high. Pendleton was named the Most Valuable Player in the National League.

The Braves won the NL West and the National League pennant. Pendleton hit .367 with two home runs in the 1991 World Series, but Minnesota beat the Braves 4–3.

For the ninth consecutive season, Cal Ripken Jr. played every single game for the Baltimore Orioles. He hit .323 (sixth behind Julio Franco's .341) with 34 home runs (José Canseco and Cecil Fielder had 44) and 114 RBIs and led the AL with 85 extra base hits and 368 total bases.

Ripken was rewarded with an All-Star selection, a Gold Glove (his first), his sixth Silver Slugger Award, and the American League's Most Valuable Player Award.

The Orioles finished the 1991 season in sixth place, 67-95, 24 games behind the division-winning Toronto Blue Jays.

In and Around Baseball 1991:

July 28: Dennis Martinez—"El Presidente"—from Grenada, Nicaragua, becomes the first foreign-born pitcher to throw a perfect game, as his Montreal Expos beat the Los Angeles Dodgers 2–0. Martinez's catcher, Ron Hassey, becomes the first (and so far the only) man to catch *two* perfect games: He also caught Len Barker's on May 15, 1981 . . . The Toronto Blue Jays become the first team to draw over four million fans in a season.

The Minnesota Twins faced the Atlanta Braves in the World Series. The Braves had made a dramatic comeback to get there: They were last in the National League in 1990, and won the NL pennant in 1991. Likewise, the Twins were last in the American League West in 1990. In 1991, they were the AL champs.

Having won Game 1 of the Fall Classic and pitched with no decision in a Game 4 won by the Braves, Twins pitcher—and St. Paul native—Jack Morris starts Game 7 facing John Smoltz. The game is scoreless through seven innings. Morris pitched a complete game, which goes 10 innings. Morris earns his second win and the Series MVP Award.

OUR 78th YEAR

78th Edition
$8.50

1993 *who's who*
in BASEBALL

LIFETIME RECORDS
Of More Than
975 PLAYERS
Plus PHOTOS

DENNIS ECKERSLEY
AL Cy Young Winner & MVP

Exclusive!
**FIRST-TIME STATS
& PHOTOS OF
EXPANSION
TEAM
PLAYERS**

BARRY BONDS
NL MVP

**HANDY
REFERENCE
GUIDE TO BATTING AND
PITCHING STATS**

GREG MADDUX
NL Cy Young Winner

1993—DENNIS ECKERSLEY, BARRY BONDS, GREG MADDUX

For the first 14 years of his 24-year career, Dennis Eckersley was a very good starting pitcher. On May 30, 1977, pitching for the Cleveland Indians, he threw the 200th no-hitter in major league history. That year he made his first of six All-Star teams.

In 1978, with the Boston Red Sox, he was a 20-game winner. But when he joined the Oakland Athletics in 1987, manager Tony La Russa made one of the best decisions of his Hall of Fame career: La Russa made Eckersley a closer. The move made "The Eck" a Hall of Famer. The next season, he led the American League with 45 saves and helped the A's win the American League pennant.

In 1992, he was an All-Star and became the seventh pitcher to win both the Cy Young and Most Valuable Player Awards in the same season, as his A's won the American League West. Eckersley led the American League with 51 saves—10 more than #2, Rick Aguilera. Over his career, he struck out 2,401 batters while walking only 738.

1992 was left fielder Barry Bonds's seventh and last season with the Pittsburgh Pirates before he spent 15 years with the San Francisco Giants.

His genes helped. His father Bobby Bonds had been an excellent outfielder for 14 years, and his cousin Reggie Jackson was quite a ballplayer too.

But whether through bloodlines, performance enhancers, natural talent, or hard work, Barry Bonds moved things to a new level. In 1992 he hit 34 home runs, 75 extra base hits, had 103 RBIs and 295 total bases, walked 127 times, scored 109 runs, was on base 279 times, and had 32 intentional walks—all league-leading stats. He also led the league in on-base and slugging percentage. Bonds stole 39 bases. He was also a very good left fielder.

Bonds won just about every award you can win in baseball: a Silver Slugger Award, a trip to the All-Star Game (one of his 13 selections), a Gold Glove (one of his eight), and selection as the Most Valuable Player in the National League—one of his record *seven* MVP Awards. But Bonds was only the third highest paid player in the NL, behind Barry Bonilla and Dwight Gooden. Bonds led the Pirates to first place in the NL East, but they lost the League Championship Series to the Atlanta Braves.

After seven years in Chicago, 1992 was Greg Maddux's last with the Cubs before signing with the Atlanta Braves as a free agent.

Maddux went out with a bang. He led the National League with 20 wins and 268 innings pitched—a personal high. He was an All-Star (one of eight selections), *The Sporting News* National League Pitcher of the Year, and won his first of four Cy Young Awards. He won a record 18 consecutive Gold Gloves.

Maddux pitched in the major leagues for 23 years, and retired after the 2008 season when he was 42. Over his Hall of Fame career, he led the National League in shutouts five times, and fewest home runs per nine innings four times. He led in putouts by a pitcher eight times and assists 12.

In and Around Baseball 1992:

For the first time, the average annual salary for a major leaguer tops $1 million . . . April 6: The Baltimore Orioles get a new ballpark and it's a gem: Oriole Park at Camden Yards opens and becomes the model for many baseball stadiums which follow . . . May 1: Rickey Henderson of the Oakland Athletics steals his 1,000th base . . . The Most Valuable Player in the July 14 All-Star Game is Ken Griffey Jr. His father Ken Sr. was the MVP of the 1980 All-Star Game—the only father and son All-Star MVP pair . . . August 19: With the debut of Bret Boone of the Seattle Mariners, the Boones become the first three-generation family to play in the big leagues: his father Bob and his grandfather Ray were major leaguers too . . . September 7: Baseball Commissioner Francis T. "Fay" Vincent Jr. resigns—forced out by owners. September 9: Robin Yount of the Milwaukee Brewers gets his 3,000th hit . . . September 20: Mickey Morandini, second baseman for the Philadelphia Phillies, turns the first unassisted triple play in 24 years . . . September 30: George Brett of the Kansas City Royals singles off the Angels Tom Fortugno for his 3,000th hit. Then he's picked off first base.

In 1992, for the first time ever, the winner of the World Series was not an American team. The Toronto Blue Jays beat the Atlanta Braves 4–2.

$5.95
£2.50 U.K.

1994 *who's who*
in BASEBALL

BARRY BONDS
NL MVP, HR & RBI Leader

LIFETIME RECORDS Of More Than **1,000 Players** Plus Photos

JACK McDOWELL
AL Cy Young Winner

GREG MADDUX
NL Cy Young Winner

FRANK THOMAS
AL MVP

HANDY REFERENCE GUIDE TO BATTING AND PITCHING STATS

1994—BARRY BONDS, FRANK THOMAS, JACK MCDOWELL, GREG MADDUX

Barry Bonds won his third Most Valuable Player Award in the National League. The San Francisco Giant left fielder led the NL in slugging and on-base percentage, in home runs for the first time with 46, and in RBIs for the only time with 123. He had 365 total bases and 43 intentional walks—both tops in the league. Bonds won a Gold Glove and a Silver Slugger Award.

Frank Thomas—"The Big Hurt"—was the second major leaguer named Frank Thomas. This one broke many of Bo Jackson's baseball records at Auburn University. He was a first-round pick by the Chicago White Sox in the 1989 draft. In 1993, the 6'5", 240-pound first baseman hit 41 homers, drove in 128 runs, batted .317, and was named Most Valuable Player in the American League.

In 1993, Thomas was an All-Star, won a Silver Slugger Award, and was named *The Sporting News* Major League Player of the Year, although he didn't lead the American League in any major stat.

In 1997, Thomas's .347 batting average made him the first White Sox player to lead the American League in batting since Luke Appling in 1936. Thomas is the only player with 20 home runs, a .300 batting average, 100 RBIs, and 100 walks for seven straight years.

In 1991 and 1992, Stanford graduate Jack McDowell led the major leagues in complete games with the Chicago White Sox with 15 and 13, but he really blossomed in 1993. That season, McDowell led the American League with 22 wins and four shutouts, losing only 10 games. He struck out 158 batters and had an ERA of 3.37. McDowell was named *The Sporting News* American League Pitcher of the Year. He made his third All-Star team and won the AL Cy Young Award.

The White Sox finished first in the AL West, and won their first trip to the postseason since 1983. But they lost the AL Championship Series to the ultimate world champion Toronto Blue Jays.

Greg Maddux, whose brother Mike pitched in the major leagues for 15 years, led the National League in many statistical categories in 1993, his first year with the Atlanta Braves: ERA (2.36), complete games (8), innings pitched (267), and batters faced (1,064). He won 20 games for the second consecutive year, won another Gold Glove, and was named *The Sporting News* NL Pitcher of the Year.

Maddux's fielding was also outstanding: he led the league in putouts for the fifth consecutive year and in assists for the third time. And he committed seven errors, the most in the league.

Maddux won his second of four consecutive National League Cy Young Awards. Surprisingly he was not an All-Star.

In and Around Baseball 1993:

Expansion! The Florida (later Miami) Marlins and the Colorado Rockies join the National League . . . April 8: In the seventh inning of a game against the New York Yankees, Cleveland Indians second baseman Carlos Baerga becomes the first player to homer from both sides of the plate *in the same inning* . . . May 26: José Canseco of the Texas Rangers misplays a long blast by the Cleveland Indians' Carlos Martinez in center field. It bounces off Canseco's head and over the fence for a home run . . . September 4: Jim Abbott of the New York Yankees, born with no right hand, no-hits the Cleveland Indians at home. Abbott has a 10-year career in the majors . . . September 7: Mark Whiten of the St. Louis Cardinals connects for four home runs against the Cincinnati Reds.

Joe Carter's two-run home run off Mitch Williams of the Philadelphia Phillies in the bottom of the ninth inning of Game 6 was just the second walk-off home run to win a World Series (Bill Mazeroski's in 1960 was the first). It was the Blue Jays' second world championship.

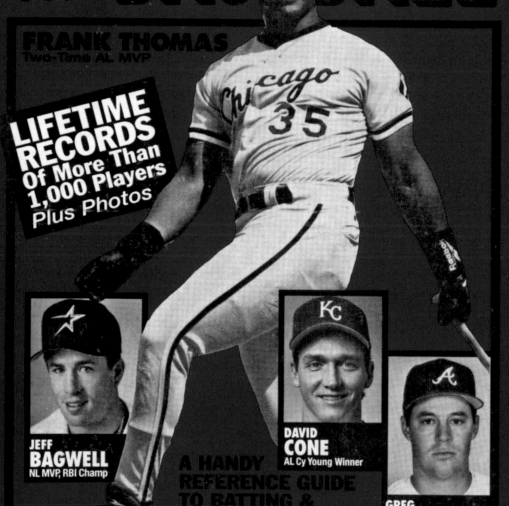

OUR 80th YEAR

$5.95

1995 *who's who in* BASEBALL

FRANK THOMAS
Two-Time AL MVP

LIFETIME RECORDS
Of More Than 1,000 Players
Plus Photos

JEFF BAGWELL
NL MVP, RBI Champ

DAVID CONE
AL Cy Young Winner

A HANDY REFERENCE GUIDE TO BATTING & PITCHING STATS

GREG MADDUX
3-Peat NL Cy Young Winner

1995—FRANK THOMAS, JEFF BAGWELL, DAVID CONE, GREG MADDUX

In 1994, Chicago White Sox first baseman Frank Thomas was the Most Valuable Player in the American League. Jeff Bagwell, the first baseman for the Houston Astros, was the MVP in the National League. In addition to 1994 being the first year that both MVPs were first basemen, Thomas and Bagwell had something else in common: They were born on *the very same day*, May 27, 1968.

Thomas led the American League in on-base and slugging percentage and in walks with 109. He batted .353, third in the AL behind Paul O'Neill's .359. He drove in 101 runs (one of 11 times he had over 100 RBIs), and scored a league-leading 106 runs. He hit 38 home runs, second in the AL behind Ken Griffey Jr.'s 40, and led the AL in extra base hits for the second time with 73 (tied with Albert Belle). He was on base 252 times, tops in the league.

He played in all 113 games of the strike-shortened season and earned a Silver Slugger Award, a trip to the All-Star Game, and his second consecutive Most Valuable Player Award—the first American Leaguer to win back-to-back MVPs since Roger Maris in 1960 and 1961.

The White Sox finished the season at the top of the AL Central, but there was no postseason because of the players' strike.

Thomas's career numbers: a .301 batting average, 1,704 RBI, an easy-to-remember 2,468 hits, 521 home runs, tied for 19th all-time with Ted Williams, 1,667 walks (10th all-time), and 0 sacrifice hits. Thomas's uniform #35 was retired by the White Sox and he was inducted into the Baseball Hall of Fame in 2014.

Jeff Bagwell, a native of Boston, was drafted by the Boston Red Sox in the fourth round of the 1989 draft out of the University of Hartford. Bagwell might have been very popular with the hometown fans in Boston, but he was traded to Houston in 1990 for Larry Anderson and spent his entire 15-year career as an Astro.

He was the National League's Rookie of the Year in 1991, but really came into his own in 1994. Bagwell hit .368 (second to Tony Gwynn's .394) in the strike-shortened season, scored 104 runs, was on base 216 times, had 116 RBIs, and 300 total bases—all best in the NL, with 39 home runs. He was *The Sporting News* Major League Player of the Year.

David Cone broke in with his hometown Kansas City Royals in 1986. After seven years with the Mets and the Blue Jays, he was back with KC in 1993. In 1994, he was 16-5 and won the American League Cy Young Award. Cone became a Yankee broadcaster after his 17-year pitching career.

In 1994, Greg Maddux of the Atlanta Braves tied with Ken Hill for the National League lead with 16 wins and had an ERA of 1.56 with 10 complete games. He was third in strikeouts and tied with Ramon Martinez for the NL lead with three shutouts—good enough for his third consecutive Cy Young Award.

In and Around Baseball 1994:

July 28: Kenny Rogers of the Texas Rangers tosses a perfect game against the California Angels. Umpire Ed Bean was working his seventh major league game behind the plate . . . September 14: Interim Commissioner Bud Selig announces that because of the major league ballplayers' strike, which started on August 12, the entire postseason, including the World Series, was cancelled. The owners wanted to eliminate salary arbitration, modify free agent eligibility, and institute a salary cap. This was the first year in a century without a World Series.

$6.95

1996 *who's who in* BASEBALL

GREG MADDUX
Four-Time NL Cy Young Winner

BARRY LARKIN
NL MVP

MO VAUGHN
AL MVP, CO-RBI LEADER

RANDY JOHNSON
AL CY YOUNG WINNER

A HANDY REFERENCE GUIDE TO BATTING & PITCHING STATS

1996—GREG MADDUX, BARRY LARKIN, MO VAUGHN, RANDY JOHNSON

Winning a Cy Young Award for *four consecutive seasons* is an achievement unmatched in baseball history. But that's what Greg Maddux did in 1992, 1993, 1994, and 1995.

Pitching for the Atlanta Braves, in 1995 he was tops in the National League with 19 wins, an ERA of 1.63, 10 complete games, and gave up the fewest runs per nine innings. He struck out 181 batters. Maddux walked one batter per nine innings. As a result, he was voted to the All-Star team. He won a Gold Glove and his fourth consecutive Cy Young Award. He was also named *The Sporting News* National League Pitcher of the Year. 1996 was Maddux's fourth consecutive appearance on the cover of *Who's Who in Baseball*.

Barry Larkin is one of 11 graduates of Cincinnati's Moeller High School to play in the major leagues.

A first-round pick of the Cincinnati Reds in 1985, Larkin, a 1984 Olympian, played only 177 games in the minors before being called up to the majors in 1986. He spent his entire 19-year career at shortstop for his hometown Reds. Although Larkin never led the National League in any major category, he was a 12-time All-Star, a three-time Gold Glove winner, and won the Silver Slugger Award nine times. His fielding percentage was always among the top four in the National League.

In 1995, Larkin stole 51 bases (379 in his career) and helped the Reds win the National League Central Division. Larkin was the NL's Most Valuable Player. The Reds were defeated by the Atlanta Braves in the NLCS.

In 1996, Larkin became the first shortstop to steal 30 bases and hit 30 home runs. He was inducted into the Baseball Hall of Fame in 2012.

Maurice "Mo" Vaughn, from Norwalk, Connecticut, was a first-round selection by Boston in 1989. The powerfully built first baseman/designated hitter spent the first eight years of his career with the Red Sox, for whom he hit 230 home runs.

In 1995, he drove in a league-leading 126 RBIs. He hit 39 home runs and scored 98 runs. Although he led the AL with 150 strikeouts, his batting average was an even .300.

Vaughn was named the Most Valuable Player in the American League as the Red Sox won the AL East, but lost the ALDS to the Cleveland Indians.

1996 was the first of Randy Johnson's record five appearances on the cover of *Who's Who in Baseball*. Until the arrival of 6'11" Jon Rauch in 2002, at 6'10" Johnson was the tallest man in the game. Selected in the second round of the 1985 draft by the Montreal Expos, "The Big Unit" pitched just 11 games for the Expos before being traded to the Seattle Mariners.

In 1995, with the Mariners (a team that also featured Alex Rodriguez and Ken Griffey Jr.), Johnson won 18 games and lost only two, for a winning percentage of .900. He also led the AL with 294 strikeouts (one of nine times he won the strikeout crown) and an ERA of 2.48.

He was an All-Star, *The Sporting News* American League Pitcher of the Year, and won his first of five AL Cy Young Awards.

Johnson had the most strikeouts per nine innings, and the best strikeout to walk ratio in the AL. He led the Mariners to their first appearance in the postseason, the American League Division Series, in which they beat the New York Yankees. But they lost the ALCS to the Cleveland Indians.

In and Around Baseball 1995:

After the near disastrous strike that shortened the 1994 season and cancelled the entire 1994 postseason, the 1995 season started late—on April 16. The season would last only 144 games . . . August 10: After Los Angeles Dodger manager Tommy Lasorda is ejected late in a game against the St. Louis Cardinals, irate fans throw their souvenir baseballs—it's "Ball Night"—onto the field, rendering it unplayable. Cards win 9–0 by forfeit, the first NL forfeit in 41 years . . . May 28: The Detroit Tigers and Chicago White Sox combine to hit a record 12 home runs . . . September 28: Montreal Expos pitcher Greg Harris pitches with both hands in the same game.

In the first year of the League Division Series, the Atlanta Braves won their first of 11 straight NL East titles. They beat the Cincinnati Reds in the NL Championship Series and won their first World Series since 1957, beating the Cleveland Indians—winner of 100 games in the strike-shortened regular season—4–2. 1995 was Cleveland's first trip to the Fall Classic since 1954.

OUR 82nd YEAR

$6.95

1997 who's who in BASEBALL

LIFETIME RECORDS Of More Than 1,000 Players Plus Photos

A HANDY REFERENCE GUIDE TO BATTING & PITCHING STATS

ALEX RODRIGUEZ AMERICAN LEAGUE BATTING CHAMPION

JOHN SMOLTZ NL CY YOUNG WINNER

PAT HENTGEN AL CY YOUNG WINNER

KEN CAMINITI NL MVP

1997—ALEX RODRIGUEZ, JOHN SMOLTZ, PAT HENTGEN, KEN CAMINITI

After fewer than 200 games in the minor leagues, New York City–born Alex Rodriguez—"A-Rod"—a first-round pick of the Seattle Mariners in the 1993 draft, was a major leaguer at 18 in 1994. In 1996, his first full season with Seattle, the 20-year-old led the American League with a career-high batting average of .358 (Rodriguez's only batting crown), 379 total bases, 54 doubles, and 141 runs scored. His 91 extra base hits were second only to Brady Anderson's 92.

Rodriguez was named to the first of his 14 All-Star teams, and won his first of 10 Silver Slugger Awards. He was *The Sporting News* Major League Player of the Year. Juan Gonzalez of the Texas Rangers was the AL Most Valuable Player. Rodriguez was the first player featured on the cover of *Who's Who in Baseball* who was not the Most Valuable Player or Cy Young Award winner since.

For 11 seasons, Rodriguez was the highest paid player in baseball and one of its biggest stars. He was suspended for the entire 2014 season because of his involvement with performance-enhancing drugs.

John Smoltz spent 20 years of his 21-year major league career pitching for the Atlanta Braves. 1996 was his best year. He led the National League in strikeouts with 276 and in wins with 24. He was tops in innings pitched, too—253.2. Because he lost only eight games, he also led in winning percentage—.750. Smoltz averaged more than a strikeout per inning. He was voted to the All-Star team and won the NL Cy Young Award.

Between 2002 and 2004, Smoltz was a relief pitcher. In 2002 he led the National League with 55 saves, but went back to starting in 2005. He led the NL in wins with 16 in 2006.

Smoltz retired after the 2009 season with 3,084 strikeouts, 210 wins, 154 saves, and an ERA of 3.33.

Right-hander Pat Hentgen had 20 wins for the Toronto Blue Jays, a league-leading 10 complete games and 265.2 innings pitched. Hentgen also led the American League by surrendering only .07 home runs per nine innings. Hentgen was *The* *Sporting News* American League Pitcher of the Year and the AL's Cy Young Award winner.

The Blue Jays finished in fourth place in the American League East, 18 games behind the New York Yankees.

Ken Caminiti won the National League Most Valuable Player Award in 1996 with the San Diego Padres—the first Padre to appear on the cover of *Who's Who in Baseball*, and the first Padre to win the MVP. Although he led the National League in only one category, sacrifice flies (tied with Dante Bichette and Rick Wilkins), Caminiti had a monster year. The third baseman had 178 hits, 40 home runs, scored 109, and drove in 130. He was second in putouts, assists, and double plays turned at third base. He was an All-Star, a Gold Glove winner, and also won a Silver Slugger Award. The Padres were swept 3–0 by the St. Louis Cardinals in the National League Division Series.

In and Around Baseball 1996:

Because of reconstruction at the Oakland Coliseum, the A's play their first six home games at Cashman Field in Las Vegas, a minor league facility . . . April 6: Working home plate in Cincinnati on Opening Day, 328-pound umpire John McSherry collapses after just seven pitches and dies . . . Mark McGwire becomes the only US Olympian to hit 50 home runs in a season. He was a member of the gold medal–winning team in 1984, and blasted 52 home runs for the Oakland A's in 1996 . . . August 16: The San Diego Padres beat the New York Mets 15–10 in an official game in Monterrey, Mexico . . . September 13: Toronto Blue Jays catcher Charlie O'Brien is the first to use a hockey goalie–style catcher's mask . . . September 17: Hideo Nomo of the Los Angeles Dodgers throws a no-hitter in the thin air of Denver's Coors Field to beat the Rockies 9–0.

The Atlanta Braves were in the postseason every year from 1991 to 2005, but they only won the Series once in that period, in 1995. In the 1996 Series the New York Yankees beat the Braves 4–2—the Yanks' first World Series victory since 1978.

1998 who's who in BASEBALL

LIFETIME RECORDS of More Than 1,000 Players
Plus Photos

A HANDY REFERENCE GUIDE TO BATTING & PITCHING STATS

PEDRO MARTINEZ
NL CY YOUNG WINNER

LARRY WALKER
NL MVP, HR LEADER

ROGER CLEMENS
AL CY YOUNG WINNER

MARK McGWIRE
MAJOR LEAGUE HOME RUN LEADER (58)

1998—MARK MCGWIRE, ROGER CLEMENS, PEDRO MARTINEZ, LARRY WALKER

On July 31, 1997, six months after his Oakland Athletics manager, Tony La Russa, signed to manage the St. Louis Cardinals, Mark McGwire was traded by Oakland to the Cardinals for three players. Getting used to National League umpires, pitchers, and stadiums did not put a crimp in McGwire's outstanding play at the plate or at first base.

Because he split the 1997 season between both leagues, McGwire didn't lead either league in any statistic. But he led the *major* leagues with 58 home runs, the third of five times he led the majors in homers. He's the second player, after Babe Ruth, to hit at least 50 homers in consecutive seasons. He was in the major league's top ten in slugging, total bases, RBI, walks, intentional walks, and extra base hits.

McGwire was an All-Star, but the Cardinals finished fourth in the National League Central Division, 11 games behind the first place Houston Astros.

Roger Clemens signed as a free agent with the Toronto Blue Jays in 1996. He dominated the American League in 1997. Clemens won the Triple Crown of Pitching: most wins—21; most strikeouts—292; and lowest ERA—2.05. He tied with Pat Hentgen for the most complete games—9, most innings pitched—264, and most shutouts—3.

Clemens was *The Sporting News* AL Pitcher of the Year and won his fourth Cy Young Award. But it didn't really matter: Clemens was the best pitcher on the worst team. The Blue Jays were last in the American League East, 22 games behind the first place Baltimore Orioles.

Pitching for the Montreal Expos, Pedro Martinez, whose brother Ramon was also a big-league pitcher, led the National League in 1997 with an ERA of only 1.90. He also led all major league pitchers with 13 complete games. Martinez averaged 11.374 Ks per nine innings—the best in the league.

Martinez was an All-Star and won the Cy Young Award in the National League. He later won two more with the Boston Red Sox. He was *The Sporting News* National League Pitcher of the Year.

Larry Walker, a native of Maple Ridge, British Columbia, was the first Canadian and the first Colorado Rockies player to appear on the cover of *Who's Who in Baseball*. In 1997 as a Rockie he became the first Canadian to win the National League Most Valuable Player Award by hitting a league-leading 49 home runs, batting .366, with 409 total bases—also tops in the NL. He was an All-Star and won both Silver Slugger and Gold Glove Awards.

The Rockies finished third in the NL West.

In and Around Baseball 1997:

Olympic Stadium in Atlanta, built for the 1996 summer games, is refurbished and turned into Turner Field, the new home of the Atlanta Braves . . . April 15: On the 50th anniversary of Jackie Robinson's first game for the Brooklyn Dodgers, Commissioner Alan "Bud" Selig announced that Robinson's uniform #42 would be retired throughout baseball. Only those players still wearing it (including Mo Vaughn of the Boston Red Sox and Mariano Rivera of the New York Yankees) would be allowed to finish their careers with #42 . . . April 19: The San Diego Padres host the first of three games against the St. Louis Cardinals at Honolulu's Aloha Stadium . . . May 11: Ted Turner, the owner of the Atlanta Braves, manages his team wearing uniform #27. The Pittsburgh Pirates beat the Braves 2–1, and Turner is reminded of the rule prohibiting any owner from managing—in uniform or out . . . June 12: Interleague play arrives, as the Texas Rangers host the San Francisco Giants in a regular season game: Giants 4, Texas 3.

Playing in their first World Series in just their fifth year of existence, the Florida (now Miami) Marlins beat the Cleveland Indians 4–3.

OUR 84th YEAR

$6.95

1999 *who's who*
in BASEBALL

LIFETIME RECORDS
of More Than 800 Players
Plus Photos

A Handy
REFERENCE
GUIDE
To Batting
& Pitching
Stats

MARK McGWIRE
Major League
Home Run
Record (70)

SAMMY SOSA
NL MVP, RBI
Leader, NL HR
Leader (66)

Home Run Heroes

1999—MARK MCGWIRE, SAMMY SOSA

In 1998, Mark McGwire of the St. Louis Cardinals and Sammy Sosa of the Chicago Cubs battled all season to see who would be the first to break Roger Maris's single-season record of 61 homers set in 1961. McGwire's 58 home runs in 1997 were just a prelude.

Along the way, McGwire broke Hack Wilson's 68-year-old National League record of 56 home runs by hitting number 57 on September 1. He tied Maris at 61 on September 7. McGwire won that race, hitting home run #62 on September 8. He went on to hit eight more for a season total of 70. The ball he hit for home run #70 was later auctioned for over three million dollars.

After a year with the Texas Rangers in 1989, Sammy Sosa was involved in a trade with the Chicago White Sox. After three years, on the South Side, he spent the next 13 years with the Chicago Cubs.

In 1998 Sosa hit 66 home runs—second only to McGwire's 70. Sosa led the National League with 158 RBI, 134 runs scored, and 416 total bases. He was also #1 in strikeouts with 171. Sosa was an All-Star and the winner of a Silver Slugger Award. He was the overwhelming choice for Most Valuable Player in the National League, leaving McGwire a distant second.

Sosa was *The Sporting News* Major League Player of the Year and also won the Roberto Clemente Humanitarian Award.

The careers (and Hall of Fame suitability) of both McGwire and Sosa were later tainted by allegations of the use of steroids and other performance-enhancing drugs.

In and around Baseball 1998:

In an unprecedented move, the Milwaukee Brewers switched from the American to the National League, giving each league an even number of teams . . . Expansion! The Arizona Diamondbacks join the National League and the Tampa Bay Devil Rays (since 2008, just Rays) join the American League. On May 6, 20-year-old Chicago Cubs pitcher Kerry Wood becomes the second pitcher (after 17-year-old Bob Feller) to strike out his age, as he strikes out 20 Houston Astros. Wood is the first National Leaguer to strike out 20 in one game . . . May 17: New York Yankee pitcher David Wells throws a perfect game beating the Minnesota Twins 4–0 at Yankee Stadium—the first perfect game by a Yankee since Don Larsen's in Game 5 of the 1956 World Series. Both Wells and Larsen attended Point Loma High School in San Diego . . . September 16: Tom Browning of the Cincinnati Reds throws a perfect game.

The San Diego Padres were the National League champions and played in their second World Series. They were swept by the New York Yankees, who won the American League East by 22 games, and won 114 regular season games.

OUR 85th YEAR

$6.95

2000 who's who in BASEBALL

LIFETIME RECORDS of More Than 800 Players *Plus Photos*

A Handy REFERENCE GUIDE To Batting & Pitching Stats

CHIPPER JONES NL MVP

IVAN RODRIGUEZ AL MVP

PEDRO MARTINEZ AL CY YOUNG WINNER

RANDY JOHNSON NL CY YOUNG WINNER

2000—CHIPPER JONES, PEDRO MARTINEZ, RANDY JOHNSON, IVAN RODRIGUEZ

Atlanta Braves third baseman Larry "Chipper" Jones won a Silver Slugger Award and was the Most Valuable Player in the National League in 1999, although he did not lead the league in any important statistical category. He was second in intentional walks (18) and tied for second place in times on base (309) and extra base hits (87). He hit 45 home runs and batted .319 with 181 hits and 110 RBIs. His Braves won the NL pennant, but they were swept by the New York Yankees in the World Series.

In 1999 Pedro Martinez led the American League with 23 wins, 313 strikeouts and an ERA of 2.07, winning the Triple Crown of Pitching. The second highest paid player in the league at a reported $11,10,000 per year, Martinez was an All-Star, *The Sporting News* American League Pitcher of the Year, and won his second AL Cy Young Award. He gave up the fewest hits and the fewest home runs per nine innings. Martinez also had the best strikeout to walk ratio (8.46) in the AL. In 1999, Martinez started the All-Star Game for the American League at Boston's Fenway Park—his home park.

Randy Johnson was on the cover of *Who's Who in Baseball* for the second time. In his first year with the Arizona Diamondbacks, he was an All-Star and won his second of four consecutive Cy Young Awards. Only four other pitchers have won the award in both leagues: Gaylord Perry, Pedro Martinez, Roy Halladay, and Roger Clemens.

Johnson was 17-9 but had a league-leading ERA of 2.48 and 364 strikeouts with 12 complete games. He had 12.059 strikeouts per nine innings, the best ratio in the league. The Diamondbacks won 100 games—the most in their history, and won the NL West, but lost the National League Division Series to the New York Mets.

Ivan Rodriguez, known as "Pudge" and "I-Rod," broke into the majors as a catcher with the Texas Rangers when he was 19.

In 1999, he caught 144 games and had a batting average of .332, seventh best in the league. He hit 35 home runs, scored 116 runs, and drove in 113 with 199 hits.

He was excellent behind the plate too, finishing second in the league in putouts, double plays turned, and assists by a catcher. Rodriguez won a Gold Glove and was chosen the American League's Most Valuable Player—only the third catcher to be so honored, and the first since Elston Howard in 1963.

The Rangers won the AL West Division, but lost to the Yankees in the ALDS.

In and Around Baseball 1999:

April 23: Fernando Tatis of the St. Louis Cardinals becomes the first player to hit two grand slams in the same inning . . . June 9: In the 12th inning, New York Mets manager Bobby Valentine is ejected by umpire Randy Marsh for arguing an interference call. He returns to the Mets dugout in an eye-black mustache, a non-Mets hat, and sunglasses. Valentine is suspended for two games and fined $8,000 . . . July 1: At the 70th All-Star Game at Fenway Park, nominees to The All-Century Team walk out onto the field. The last player introduced is Red Sox legend Ted Williams, who throws out the ceremonial first pitch to Carlton Fisk. During the game, hometown hero Pedro Martinez strikes out Barry Larkin, Larry Walker, Sammy Sosa, Mark McGwire, and Jeff Bagwell . . . July 18: Yogi Berra Day at Yankee Stadium. After a long estrangement from owner George M. Steinbrenner III, Yogi was welcomed back to Yankee Stadium. Don Larsen, Yogi's battery mate during Larsen's perfect Game 5 of the 1956 World Series, threw out the first pitch. To catch it, Berra borrowed Yankee catcher Joe Girardi's mitt. Some Yogi magic must have rubbed off: starting pitcher David Cone throws the first interleague perfect game against the Montreal Expos . . . July 15: 57 major league umpires submit their resignations. Some were later rescinded; 22 were accepted. The umpire's union was decertified and a new union formed . . . Mark McGwire gets his 500th home run and two players get their 3,000th hits in 1999: Tony Gwynn and Wade Boggs . . . September 1: Mark McGwire surpasses Lou Gehrig's 60-year-old record of most home runs by a first baseman when he hits his 52nd homer of the year . . . September 11: Eric Milton of the Minnesota Twins pitches a no-hitter . . . In 1999, Mark McGwire becomes the first player with at least 100 hits to have more RBIs (147) than hits (145).

After beating the Boston Red Sox 4–1 in the AL Championship Series, the New York Yankees defend their 1998 world championship by sweeping the Atlanta Braves in the World Series.

2001 *who's who*
in BASEBALL

LIFETIME RECORDS
of More Than
700 Players
Plus Photos

A Handy
REFERENCE
GUIDE
To Batting &
Pitching
Stats

JASON
GIAMBI
AL MVP

JEFF
KENT
NL MVP

RANDY
JOHNSON
NL CY YOUNG
WINNER

PEDRO
MARTINEZ
AL CY YOUNG WINNER

2001—PEDRO MARTINEZ, JASON GIAMBI, JEFF KENT, RANDY JOHNSON

Pedro Martinez was on the cover of *Who's Who in Baseball* for the second time. In 2000, the 5'11" Red Sox right-hander was 18-6 with a league-leading ERA of 1.74 and 284 strikeouts. He was an All-Star and won the American League Cy Young Award—his third.

Jason Giambi led the majors with 137 walks, hit .333, with an on-base percentage of .477—tops in the league—and smacked 29 home runs, second in the American League to Troy Glaus's 47. He was an All-Star, and won the Hutch Award and his only Most Valuable Player Award.

The first baseman led Oakland to first place in the AL West, but they lost in the Division Series to the ultimate world champions, the New York Yankees.

Jeff Kent, the San Francisco Giants second baseman from Bellflower, California, was the Most Valuable Player in the National League, although he didn't lead the league in any major statistic. He batted .334 with 33 homers and 41 doubles.

Kent hit 351 home runs as a second baseman (377 altogether), the most at that position. He was the first second baseman to drive in 100 runs in six consecutive years, 1997–2002.

The Giants won the AL West, but lost the Division Series to the New York Mets, who went on to lose the Subway Series to the Yankees.

Randy Johnson had one of his finest years in 2000, and appeared on the cover of *Who's Who in Baseball* for the third consecutive time. Pitching for the Arizona Diamondbacks, he was 19-7 with a league-leading winning percentage of .731 and eight complete games. He was also #1 with 347 strikeouts. The Big Unit was an All-Star and won his third Cy Young Award. But the Diamondbacks finished in third place behind the San Francisco Giants.

In and Around Baseball 2000:

March 29: The New York Mets and the Chicago Cubs open the baseball season with a game in Japan's Tokyo Dome . . . April 15: Cal Ripken Jr. gets his 3,000th hit . . . May 29: Randy Velarde of the Oakland Athletics turns an unassisted triple play against the New York Yankees . . . July 8: The New York Mets and New York Yankees play a unique doubleheader—one game at Shea Stadium, and one game at Yankee Stadium—the first split twinbill since 1903. In the second game, Yankees pitcher Roger Clemens beans Mets catcher Mike Piazza, giving him a concussion . . . When the two faced each other that year in the World Series, Piazza broke his bat on a slow-roller up the first base line. Half the bat headed toward the mound. Clemens picked it up and threw it at Piazza. He was fined $50,000 . . . December 11: Shortstop Alex Rodriguez signs a 10-year contract with the Texas Rangers for a reported $22.5 million per year, making him the highest paid professional athlete ever.

In the Subway Series, the New York Yankees beat the New York Mets 4–1 to win their third consecutive World Series, their fourth in five years. 🔵

$8.95

2002 *who's who* in BASEBALL

LIFETIME RECORDS of More Than 700 Players
Plus Photos

A Handy REFERENCE GUIDE To Batting & Pitching Stats

RANDY JOHNSON
NL Cy Young Winner, ERA Leader, Co-World Series MVP

ICHIRO SUZUKI
AL MVP, Batting Champion, Rookie of the Year

BARRY BONDS
RECORD SETTING: 73 HOME RUNS, SLUGGING PCT, WALKS. NL MVP

2002—BARRY BONDS, RANDY JOHNSON, ICHIRO SUZUKI

Barry Bonds of the San Francisco Giants won his fourth National League Most Valuable Player award. He hit career home run #500 on April 16, one of an all-time record 73 he hit that season (#73 came on October 7, the last day of the season). He hit .328 and walked a league-leading 177 times, including 35 intentional walks.

Randy Johnson made his record fourth cover of *Who's Who in Baseball*. He won his fourth Cy Young Award with the Arizona Diamondbacks, going 21-6 (only Matt Morris and Curt Schilling had more wins—22) and leading the National League in ERA (2.49) and strikeouts (372).

After nine years as a star with the Orix Blue Wave in the Japanese Pacific League, Ichiro Suzuki, a native of Nichi Kasugai-gun, Aichi, Japan, burst on to the American baseball scene in 2001. He was the first Japanese player to appear on the cover of *Who's Who in Baseball*. The Seattle Mariners right fielder became the second player (after Fred Lynn in 1975) to win both the Rookie of the Year and Most Valuable Player Awards *in the same year*. Playing in 157 games, Ichiro (he preferred to be called by his first name, and that's what appeared on the back of his uniform) led the American League in batting average (.350), at-bats (692), plate appearances (738), hits (242), and stolen bases (56). He was an All-Star, and won a Gold Glove and a Silver Slugger Award.

Ichiro led the AL in singles for 10 straight years and in putouts by a right fielder for seven. In mid-2012, he was traded to the New York Yankees.

In and Around Baseball 2001:

April 2, 2001, Opening Day: New York Yankees pitcher Roger Clemens strikes out Joe Randa of the Kansas City Royals in the top of the ninth inning, Clemens's 3,409th career strikeout, breaking Walter Johnson's 88-year-old record for most strikeouts in the history of the American League . . . April 4: Hideo Nomo of the Boston Red Sox throws a no-hitter, becoming the fourth man (after Cy Young, Jim Bunning, and Nolan Ryan) to pitch no-hitters in both leagues . . . All major league games between September 11 and September 17 were cancelled following the terrorist attacks on New York's World Trade Center, the Pentagon, and Shanksville, Pennsylvania. Games resumed on September 18 after the longest break in a season since World War I . . . October 4: Tim Raines Sr. and Jr. both play the outfield for the Baltimore Orioles—the second father-and-son pair to play together . . . October 4: Rickey Henderson of the San Diego Padres scores run #2,246, breaking Ty Cobb's record for runs scored in a career . . . October 30: President George W. Bush tosses a perfect strike as he throws out the first pitch of the World Series from the mound at New York's Yankee Stadium . . . September 3: Rookie Bud Smith of the St. Louis Cardinals throws a no-hitter against the San Diego Padres.

Randy Johnson won Games 1, 6, and 7 in the World Series between the Arizona Diamondbacks—in just their fourth year of existence—and the New York Yankees and was voted the MVP of the Fall Classic—his only World Series. Because all major league games were suspended for a week after the terrorist attacks (see above), the Series was the first to stretch into November. Game 4, in New York, started on October 31. By the time Derek Jeter came to bat after midnight in the 10th inning, the Yankee Stadium message board said: "ATTENTION FANS: WELCOME TO NOVEMBER BASEBALL!" Jeter hit a walk-off home run to win the game, but the Diamondbacks won the Series 4–3.

2003—RANDY JOHNSON, BARRY BONDS, MIGUEL TEJADA

Randy Johnson appeared on the cover of *Who's Who in Baseball* for a record fifth time and for the fourth time in a row. Playing for the Arizona Diamondbacks, Johnson won the Triple Crown of Pitching—leading the National League with 24 wins, 334 strikeouts, and an ERA of 2.32. It was the first NL Triple Crown of Pitching since Dwight Gooden did it in 1985. Johnson also led the NL in strikeouts per nine innings, innings pitched (260), and complete games (8). He pitched four shutouts.

Johnson's mound heroics didn't help his team much. Although Arizona won the NL West, they were defeated by the St. Louis Cardinals in the Division Series. Nevertheless, Johnson was an All-Star and won his fifth Cy Young Award, including four in a row.

Johnson's career numbers are impressive: 303 wins, 4,875 strikeouts—#2 all time, and an ERA of 3.29.

In 2002, the 37-year-old Barry Bonds hit .370, tops in the National League, with a league-leading 198 bases on balls including 68 intentional walks. He drove in 110 runs for the San Francisco Giants, who finished second in the National League West behind Arizona. The Giants were the NL Wild Card team and won the NL pennant, but lost the World Series 4–3 to another California team, the Anaheim Angels.

Bonds was an All-Star and Silver Slugger Award winner and won his fifth NL Most Valuable Player Award.

Miguel Tejada spent 16 years playing shortstop in the major leagues. He was an All-Star in 2002, when he was with the Oakland A's. He led the league in assists and won the MVP in the American League.

In and Around Baseball 2002:

April 30: New York Mets pitcher Al Leiter beats the Arizona Diamondbacks, becoming the first pitcher in the majors to defeat all 30 big-league teams . . . May 2: Mike Cameron of the Seattle Mariners hits four home runs against the Chicago White Sox . . . July 9: The All-Star Game in Milwaukee ends in an 11-inning tie as both teams run out of pitchers . . . May 23: Shawn Green of the Los Angeles Dodgers hits four homers against the Milwaukee Brewers . . . August 9: Barry Bonds hits career home run #600.

The Anaheim Angels came into the American League as an expansion team in 1961. In 2002 they won the American League pennant as the Wild Card team and reached the World Series for the first time. They beat the San Francisco Giants—the NL Wild Card team—4 games to 3. 🌑

$9.95

2004 *who's who* in **BASEBALL**

LIFETIME RECORDS
of More Than 750 Players
Plus Photos

A Handy Reference Guide To Batting & Pitching Stats

ERIC GAGNE
NL Cy Young Winner

ROY HALLADAY
AL Cy Young Winner

ALEX RODRIGUEZ
AL MVP, Home Run Leader

BARRY BONDS
6 Time NL MVP

2004—BARRY BONDS, ERIC GAGNE, ROY HALLADAY, ALEX RODRIGUEZ

Barry Bonds of the San Francisco Giants made his third appearance on the cover of *Who's Who in Baseball*. He led the majors with 148 walks, including a majors-leading 61 intentional walks. Bonds is the first National Leaguer to win the MVP four, five, six, and finally seven times. He was an All-Star and won a Silver Slugger Award. Bonds was third in the National League with a batting average of .341. His on-base percentage and slugging percentage were both #1 in the NL. He hit 45 home runs, second in the league to Jim Thome's 47.

The Giants won the NL West, but lost in the Division Series to the Florida Marlins.

Montreal native Eric Gagne—the second Canadian to appear on the cover of *Who's Who in Baseball*—saved a league-leading 55 games for the Los Angeles Dodgers with an ERA of 1.20 and won the Cy Young Award in the National League. He was the Rolaids Relief Pitcher of the Year in the NL, as well as *The Sporting News* NL Pitcher of the Year.

Harry Leroy "Roy" "Doc" Halladay led the American League with 22 wins in 2003, with only seven losses. The 6'6" Toronto Blue Jay right-hander also led in innings pitched (266), batters faced (1,071), and complete games (9). He was an All-Star and won the American League Cy Young Award. Halladay was selected as *The Sporting News* AL Pitcher of the Year.

Alex Rodriguez appeared on the cover of *Who's Who in Baseball* for the second time. In his third year with the Texas Rangers, he hit .298 and led both leagues with 47 home runs and 124 runs scored. He had 118 RBIs and a league-best slugging percentage of .600. He was an All-Star at shortstop, a Gold Glove and Silver Slugger Award winner, and won the Most Valuable Player Award in the American League—his first of three. But the Rangers finished with a 71-91 record, last in the AL West, 25 games out of first place. Rodriguez's achievements were later tainted by his admission of steroid use from 2001 to 2003.

In and Around Baseball 2003:

June 13: Pitching for the New York Yankees, Roger Clemens reaches two milestones in one game: 4,000 strikeouts and 300 wins . . . July 29: Bill Mueller of the Boston Red Sox hits grand slams from both sides of the plate plus another home run . . . August 10: Rafael Furcal of the Atlanta Braves turns an unassisted triple play against the St. Louis Cardinals . . . September 25: Blue Jays slugger Carlos Delgado smacks four home runs in a game against the Tampa Bay Rays . . . Victor Zambrano of the Tampa Bay Rays wins the *reverse* Triple Crown of Pitching, leading the AL with 106 walks, 115 wild pitches, and 20 hit batters—the first pitcher to accomplish this dubious feat in 59 years . . . The same year, the Detroit Tigers Ramon Santiago "won" the "reverse Triple Crown" of batting: 2 home runs, 29 RBIs, and a batting average of .225—all the worst in the AL . . . This year's All-Star Game is the first one that really means something besides bragging rights: From now on, the league which wins the All-Star Game will have home-field advantage in the World Series. . . . June 11: Six Houston Astros pitchers combine for a no-hitter.

In 2003, the Florida Marlins were the NL's Wild Card team. They won only 91 games in the regular season, but they wound up as NL champions, and beat the Yankees 4–2 in the World Series.

2005 who's who in BASEBALL

LIFETIME RECORDS
of More Than **750 Players**
Plus Photos

A Handy Reference Guide To Batting & Pitching Stats

BARRY BONDS
NL MVP, Batting Champion

ICHIRO SUZUKI
AL Batting Champion
Record-Breaking 262 Hits

JOHAN SANTANA
AL Cy Young Winner, ERA Leader

ROGER CLEMENS
SEVEN TIME CY YOUNG WINNER

2005—ROGER CLEMENS, JOHAN SANTANA, ICHIRO SUZUKI, BARRY BONDS

In 2004, his first year with the Houston Astros in the National League, 41-year-old Roger Clemens won his record seventh Cy Young Award. He won 18 games—second to teammate Roy Oswalt's 20—and lost only four, with a league-leading winning percentage of .818. Clemens struck out 218 (fifth behind Randy Johnson's 290). He was an All-Star again. The Astros finished in second place, 13 games behind the St. Louis Cardinals, but they were the NL's Wild Card team.

The Astros beat the Atlanta Braves in the NLDS—Clemens got a win—but lost the National League Championship Series 4–3 to the Cardinals. Clemens was 1-1.

Johan Santana won the Cy Young Award in the American League. The Venezuela-born Twins left-hander led the league with 265 strikeouts and a 2.61 ERA. He won 20 games, but missed the Triple Crown of Pitching because Curt Schilling won 21. Santana won it in 2006.

Ichiro Suzuki of the Seattle Mariners had 262 hits, the most ever in a single season, breaking George Sisler's 85-year-old record of 257 set in 1920. Suzuki hit .372 in 2004—tops in both leagues.

Suzuki was also tops in the AL with 19 intentional walks. He was an All-Star and won a Gold Glove.

Barry Bonds of the San Francisco Giants hit his 700th career home run on September 17, 2004, off Jake Peavy of the San Diego Padres. Bonds hit .362 and was the National League batting champ. He added another 45 home runs and 120 intentional walks and was voted the NL's Most Valuable Player for a record seventh time. The Giants finished two games behind the Los Angeles Dodgers.

In and Around Baseball 2004:

March 11: Petco Park, the new home of the San Diego Padres, opens . . . May 18: 40-year-old Randy Johnson of the Arizona Diamondbacks becomes the oldest man to pitch a perfect game. He beat the Atlanta Braves 2–0 . . . June 20: Ken Griffey Jr. hits his 500th home run . . . August 7: Chicago Cubs pitcher Greg Maddux wins his 300th game.

The Boston Red Sox ended 86 years of frustration (and cursing) by sweeping the St. Louis Cardinals to win their first World Series since 1918. In the immortal words of Red Sox broadcaster Joe Castiglione, "Can you believe it?" Elation reigns in New England and throughout Red Sox Nation.

OUR 91st YEAR

$9.95

2006 *who's who in* BASEBALL

LIFETIME RECORDS of More Than 750 Players *Plus Photos*

A Handy Reference Guide To Batting & Pitching Stats

ALEX RODRIGUEZ
AL MVP, AL HOME RUN LEADER

BARTOLO COLON
AL Cy Young Winner

CHRIS CARPENTER
NL Cy Young Winner

ALBERT PUJOLS
NL MVP

2006—ALEX RODRIGUEZ, BARTOLO COLON, CHRIS CARPENTER, ALBERT PUJOLS

Alex Rodriguez made his third appearance on the cover of *Who's Who in Baseball*. For the third time, he played in all 162 games, mostly at third base for the New York Yankees. A-Rod led the American League with 48 home runs, 124 runs scored, 301 times on base, a .610 on-base percentage, and a .610 slugging percentage. He was an All-Star and Silver Slugger Award winner, and won his second Most Valuable Player award—his first had been in 2003 at shortstop with the Texas Rangers. He's only the second American Leaguer to win the MVP at two different positions (Robin Yount was the first at shortstop and outfield). For the fourth year, Rodriguez was the highest paid player in the game.

Although the Yankees and the Boston Red Sox finished the season with identical 95-67 records, because the Yankees had prevailed in head-to-head contests, the Yankees won the AL East, and Boston won the AL Wild Card. Both teams lost in the ALDS.

Bartolo Colon won the American League Cy Young Award in 2005. The Los Angeles Angels of Anaheim pitcher led the AL with 21 wins and was an All-Star.

St. Louis Cardinals pitcher Chris Carpenter, from Exeter, New Hampshire, won the Cy Young Award in the National League. Carpenter was also *The Sporting News* NL Pitcher of the Year. He won 21 games (second only to Dontrelle Willis's 22) and lost only five with seven complete games. The Cardinals won the NL Central and the Division Series, but lost the NLCS to the Houston Astros.

Albert Pujols won the first of his three Most Valuable Player Awards in the National League. He was third in the NL with 41 home runs and 129 runs scored. He also led both leagues with 27 intentional walks.

In and Around Baseball 2005:

In 2004, the Montreal Expos drew just 748,550 fans, averaging about 9,300 per game. Rather than just folding the team, the National League moved it to Washington, DC, where it became the Washington Nationals in 2005. Washington had been without a major league team since the second Senators team left in 1971 to become the Texas Rangers . . . March 17: Mark McGwire invokes his Fifth Amendment rights before an 11-hour House subcommittee hearing on steroid use. Rafael Palmeiro and Sammy Sosa (accompanied by his lawyer and an interpreter) deny using steroids . . . August 1: Palmeiro is suspended for 10 days for using Stanozolol, a steroid, which he continues to deny . . . August 31: Florida Marlin Jeremy Hermida pinch-hits a grand slam in his first big-league at-bat.

The Chicago White Sox sweep the Houston Astros (playing in their first Series) in the World Series—the first White Sox championship since 1917. They hadn't been in the Series since 1959.

OUR 93rd YEAR

$9.95

2008 *who's who*
in BASEBALL

LIFETIME RECORDS
of More Than
770 Players
Plus Photos

A Handy
Reference
Guide To
Batting &
Pitching
Stats

ALEX RODRIGUEZ
AL MVP, Home Run,
RBI Leader

JAKE PEAVY
NL CY Young,
ERA Leader,
Most Wins
and Strikeouts

C.C. SABATHIA
AL CY Young

JIMMY ROLLINS
NL MVP

0 27172 02736 9

2008—ALEX RODRIGUEZ, C.C. SABATHIA, JIMMY ROLLINS, JAKE PEAVY

At age 31, Alex Rodriguez proved that he was still one of the best in the game. The New York Yankee third baseman hit 54 home runs, scored 143, and drove in 156—all league-leading numbers. He was an All-Star, won a Silver Slugger Award, and won the American League's Most Valuable Player Award—his third. He was also #1 in total bases, times on base, slugging, and on-base percentage. Rodriguez was *The Sporting News* Major League Player of the Year and won the American League Hank Aaron Award for the fourth time.

In the postseason, the Yankees finished second in the American League East, behind the Boston Red Sox. The Yankees were the Wild Card team. New York lost 3–1 to Cleveland in the ALDS.

Carsten Charles "C.C." Sabathia won the Cy Young Award in 2007 with the Cleveland Indians. The 6'7", 285-pound southpaw was the first Cleveland pitcher to win the award since Gaylord Perry in 1972, 35 years before. Sabathia was 19-7, started the most games (34), pitched the most innings (241), and faced the most batters (975) in the American League. The Indians reached the ALCS and led the Red Sox 3–1, but the Bosox came back to win the next three games to win the AL pennant.

Jimmy Rollins, a second-round draft pick by the Philadelphia Phillies in 1996, hit 41 home runs and a league-leading 20 triples in 2007. The Phillies shortstop was selected as the Most Valuable Player in the National League. The Phillies won the NL East, but were swept in the Division Series by the Colorado Rockies.

San Diego Padres pitcher Jake Peavy won the Triple Crown of Pitching in the National League. He was tops in wins (19), strikeouts (240), and ERA (2.54). He was *The Sporting News* National League Pitcher of the Year and won the NL Cy Young Award.

In and Around Baseball 2007:

Major League Baseball issues a report linking 47 players to performance-enhancing drugs . . . Barry Bonds is indicted for perjury and obstruction of justice in San Francisco in connection with the Balco investigation . . . April 18: Mark Buehrle of the Chicago White Sox throws a no-hitter against the Texas Rangers . . . June 5: Trevor Hoffman of the San Diego Padres is the first pitcher to record 500 saves . . . June 12: Justin Verlander of the Detroit Tigers throws a no-hitter against the Milwaukee Brewers . . . July 10: In the Midsummer Classic, Ichiro Suzuki of the Seattle Mariners hits the first inside-the-park home run in All-Star Game history, helping the AL to a 5–4 victory. Suzuki was named the game's MVP . . . June 28: Frank Thomas of the Toronto Blue Jays hits his 500th career home run . . . June 28: The Houston Astros' Craig Biggio gets his 3,000th hit . . . August 4: At 32, Alex Rodriguez is the youngest player to hit his 500th career home run . . . August 7: Bonds hits his 756th career home run, breaking Hank Aaron's record of 755 . . . August 21: The Texas Rangers beat the Baltimore Orioles 30–3—the first modern team to score 30 runs in a game . . . September 1: In his second major league start, Clay Buchholz of the Boston Red Sox throws a no-hitter to beat the Baltimore Orioles 10–0.

The Boston Red Sox sweep the Colorado Rockies 4–0 to win the World Series, their second championship of the 21st century.

OUR 94th YEAR

$9.95

2009 *who who*
in BASEBALL®

#49

LIFETIME RECORDS
of More Than
775 Players
Plus Photos

ALBERT
PUJOLS
NL MVP

A Handy
Reference
Guide to
Batting &
Pitching
Stats

CLIFF LEE
AL Cy Young,
ERA Leader,
Most Wins

TIM
LINCECUM
NL Cy Young,
Most Strikeouts

DUSTIN
PEDROIA
AL MVP

2009—ALBERT PUJOLS, CLIFF LEE, TIM LINCECUM, DUSTIN PEDROIA

While 2009 is the second appearance by Albert Pujols of the St. Louis Cardinals on the cover of *Who's Who in Baseball*, it is his first as the main photograph. He hit 37 home runs, batted .357 (second in the league), drove in 116 runs, and scored 100. He led the National League with 342 total bases and 34 intentional walks. He was an All-Star, a Silver Slugger Award winner, and won his second NL Most Valuable Player Award, as well as the Roberto Clemente Humanitarian Award. He was *The Sporting News* National League Player of the Year.

Cliff Lee of the Cleveland Indians won the Cy Young Award in the American League with 170 strikeouts, a league-leading 22 wins, and an ERA of 2.54.

Tim Lincecum, a first-round draft pick by the San Francisco Giants in 2006, was 6-0 in his 13 minor league games. By 2007, he was pitching in the majors. In 2008, the 5'11", 170-pound Lincecum won his first of two back-to-back National League Cy Young Awards. He led the NL with a .783 winning percentage (18-5), and 265 strikeouts.

Dustin Pedroia, the 5'8", 165-pound sparkplug of the Boston Red Sox, was the American League Rookie of the Year in 2007. In 2008, he was the AL's Most Valuable Player. Pedroia led the AL with 213 hits, 54 doubles, and 118 runs scored, but his team lost the American League Championship Series to the Tampa Bay Rays.

In and Around Baseball 2008:

The Major League Players Association and Major League Baseball agree on a new drug testing program . . . March 25: The 2008 season opens with a Boston Red Sox–Oakland Athletics game in Japan's Tokyo Dome. After two games in Japan, the teams return to the USA to finish spring training . . . May 12: Asdrubal Cabrera of the Cleveland Indians turns an unassisted triple play . . . May 19: Boston's Jon Lester pitches a no-hitter against the Kansas City Royals . . . June 9: Ken Griffey Jr. of the Cincinnati Reds hits his 600th career home run.

The Philadelphia Phillies beat the Tampa Bay Rays 4–1 in the World Series, their first victory since 1980. It was the Rays' first appearance in the Fall Classic.

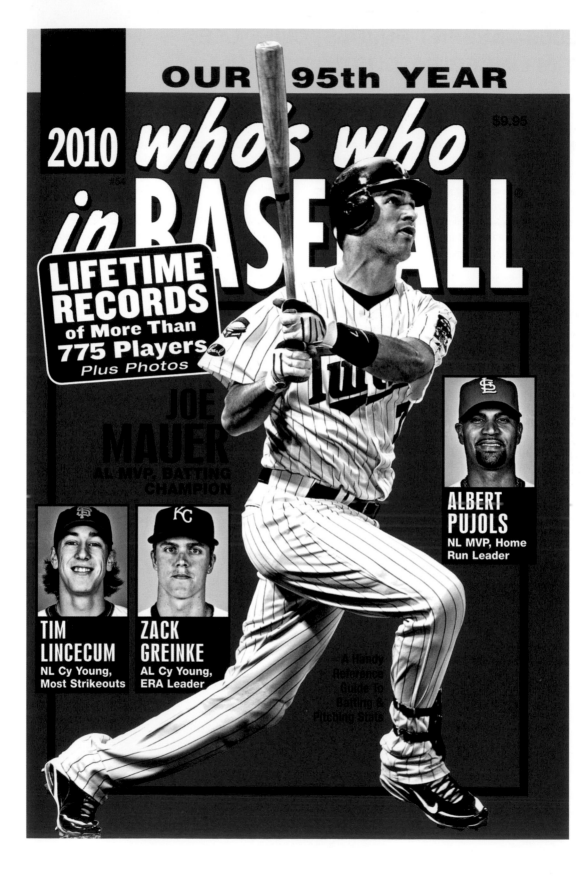

OUR 95th YEAR

$9.95

2010 *who's who*

#54

in BASEBALL®

LIFETIME RECORDS
of More Than
775 Players
Plus Photos

JOE
MAUER
AL MVP, BATTING
CHAMPION

ALBERT
PUJOLS
NL MVP, Home
Run Leader

TIM
LINCECUM
NL Cy Young,
Most Strikeouts

ZACK
GREINKE
AL Cy Young,
ERA Leader

A Handy
Reference
Guide To
Batting &
Pitching Stats

2010—JOE MAUER, TIM LINCECUM, ZACK GREINKE, ALBERT PUJOLS

In 2006, Joe Mauer of the Minnesota Twins (a graduate of the same St. Paul, Minnesota high school as Hall of Famer Paul Molitor) hit .347 and became the first catcher to win the American League batting crown. In 2009, he hit .365 and won his third AL batting title in four years and was chosen the AL's Most Valuable Player. His on-base percentage (.444) and slugging percentage (.587) were the best in the AL. He also won a Gold Glove and a Silver Slugger Award. His Twins won the AL Central Division, but were swept by the New York Yankees in the ALDS.

Tim Lincecum of the San Francisco Giants was on the cover of *Who's Who in Baseball* for the second consecutive year. He went 15-7 with a league-leading four complete games and 261 strikeouts. His ERA was 2.48, second in the National League. Lincecum won the NL Cy Young Award for the second year in a row. He was also *The Sporting News* National League Pitcher of the Year. But the Giants finished third in the NL West.

Zack Greinke of the Kansas City Royals was just the second Kansas City Royal to appear on the cover of *Who's Who in Baseball* after George Brett.

Greinke was 16-8 and led the American League with an ERA of 2.16. He gave up .4 home runs per nine innings, also the best in the AL. Greinke won the AL Cy Young Award. But his efforts didn't help, as his Royals finished tied for last in the AL Central.

Albert Pujols made his third appearance on the cover of *Who's Who in Baseball*. He led the National League with 47 home runs. He also led in intentional walks (44), runs scored (124), and total bases (374). Pujols won his second consecutive National League Most Valuable Player Award, his third overall. His Cardinals ran away with the NL Central Division, winning it by 7½ games.

In and Around Baseball 2009:

June 4: Randy Johnson of the San Francisco Giants gets his 300th career win . . . July 23: Although catcher Ramón Castro had never caught pitcher Mark Buehrle of the Chicago White Sox before, it seemed to work out: Buehrle pitched a perfect game as Chicago beat the Tampa Bay Rays 5–0.

The Yankees beat the Philadelphia Phillies in the World Series—their 27th world championship, and their first since 2000.

2011 *who's who*

$9.95

in BASEBALL

LIFETIME RECORDS of More Than **775 Players** Plus Photos

ROY HALLADAY
NL CY YOUNG
MOST WINS
PERFECT GAME

A Handy Reference Guide to Batting & Pitching Stats

JOSH HAMILTON
AL MVP, Batting Champion

JOEY VOTTO
NL MVP

FELIX HERNANDEZ
AL Cy Young, ERA Leader

2011—ROY HALLADAY, JOSH HAMILTON, JOEY VOTTO, FÉLIX HERNANDEZ

Philadelphia Phillies pitcher Roy "Doc" Halladay threw the twentieth perfect game on May 29, 2010, against the Florida Marlins. He had the most wins (21) in the National League, had nine complete games and four shutouts, and won his second National League Cy Young Award.

The Phillies won the NL East, but lost the NLCS to the San Francisco Giants.

Josh Hamilton of the Texas Rangers batted .359 to win the American League batting crown, hit 32 home runs, drove in 100 runs, and led the league in slugging. He was *The Sporting News* Major League Player of the Year and the AL Most Valuable Player.

Toronto native Joey Votto of the Cincinnati Reds was the Most Valuable Player in the National League. He had 37 home runs, batted .324, and led the NL in slugging and on-base percentage.

"King" Félix Hernandez from Carabobo, Venezuela, led the American League with an ERA of 2.27. Pitching for the Seattle Mariners, he led the AL with 249.2 innings pitched and faced 1,001 batters, the most in the AL. Hernandez won the Cy Young Award.

In and Around Baseball 2010:

May 9: The first complete game pitched by Dallas Braden of the Oakland Athletics was a perfect game on Mother's Day. He beat the Tampa Bay Rays, who had the best record in the majors at that time . . . June 2: In what would have been the final out of the perfect game pitched by Armando Galarraga of the Detroit Tigers, umpire Jim Joyce calls Jason Donald safe at first base. Replays clearly show that Donald was out. Joyce apologizes for missing the call, but it stands . . . June 27: Pitching for the Philadelphia Phillies, 47-year-old Jamie Moyer breaks Robin Roberts's record by surrendering his 506th career home run . . . September 7: Milwaukee Brewers pitcher Trevor Hoffman becomes the first pitcher to record 600 saves.

Playing in their first World Series, the Texas Rangers faced the San Francisco Giants. The Giants won 4–1, their first world championship in 56 years—when the *New York* Giants won in 1954.

OUR 97th YEAR

$9.95

2012 *who's who*

#62

in BASEBALL ®

JUSTIN VERLANDER
AL Cy Young, AL MVP,
AL ERA Leader,
Most Wins & Strikeouts

CLAYTON KERSHAW
NL Cy Young,
ERA Leader,
Most Strikeouts

RYAN BRAUN
NL MVP

A Handy Reference
Guide To Batting
& Pitching Stats

2012—JUSTIN VERLANDER, CLAYTON KERSHAW, RYAN BRAUN

Justin Verlander, the first major leaguer from Manakin Sabot, Virginia, was the Tigers' second pick in the 2004 draft out of Old Dominion University. The 6'5" right-hander was 17-9 in 2006 and was the American League Rookie of the Year.

In 2011, Verlander won the Triple Crown of Pitching for the Detroit Tigers: He led the American League with 24 wins, 250 strikeouts, and an ERA of 2.40. He lost only five games and led the AL with a winning percentage of .828 and 251 innings pitched. He was the unanimous Cy Young Award winner and was the AL Most Valuable Player. Verlander was also *The Sporting News* American League Pitcher of the Year. His Tigers ran away with the AL Central Division, winning it by 15 games.

Clayton Kershaw of the Los Angeles Dodgers emerged as one of the best pitchers in the National League. In 2011, he won the Triple Crown of Pitching, leading the NL with 21 wins, 248 strikeouts, and an ERA of 2.28.

Kershaw was the first Dodger pitcher to appear on the cover of *Who's Who in Baseball* since Fernando Valenzuela in 1982.

2011 was the first time since Walter Johnson and Dazzy Vance did it in 1924 and only the third time in history that pitchers won the Triple Crown of Pitching in both leagues (Justin Verlander in the AL and Kershaw in the NL).

But the Dodgers won only 82 games in 2011 and finished third in the NL West.

The Milwaukee Brewers' Ryan Braun, nicknamed "The Hebrew Hammer" (because he's half Jewish and averages 35 home runs per season), had 33 home runs, 187 hits, and led the National League in slugging percentage (.597) in 2011. He was an All-Star and Silver Slugger Award winner and was the Most Valuable Player in the NL. The Brewers won the NL Central Division by six games.

In 2012 Braun was suspended after a positive drug test, but he denied using steroids and the ruling was overturned on a technicality. In 2013 the Biogenesis scandal linked Braun to steroids again and this time the suspension stuck; he admitted his use of performance-enhancing drugs and apologized for lying about it the previous year.

In and Around Baseball 2011:

August 15: Jim Thome of the Minnesota Twins hits the 600th home run of his career.

The Texas Rangers repeat as American League Champions and face the St. Louis Cardinals in the World Series. In the last of manager Tony La Russa's 35 seasons as a manager before his retirement and election to the Baseball Hall of Fame, his Cardinals beat the Rangers 4–3 in the World Series. La Russa wins the American League Manager of the Year four times. His teams won three world championships and six pennants.

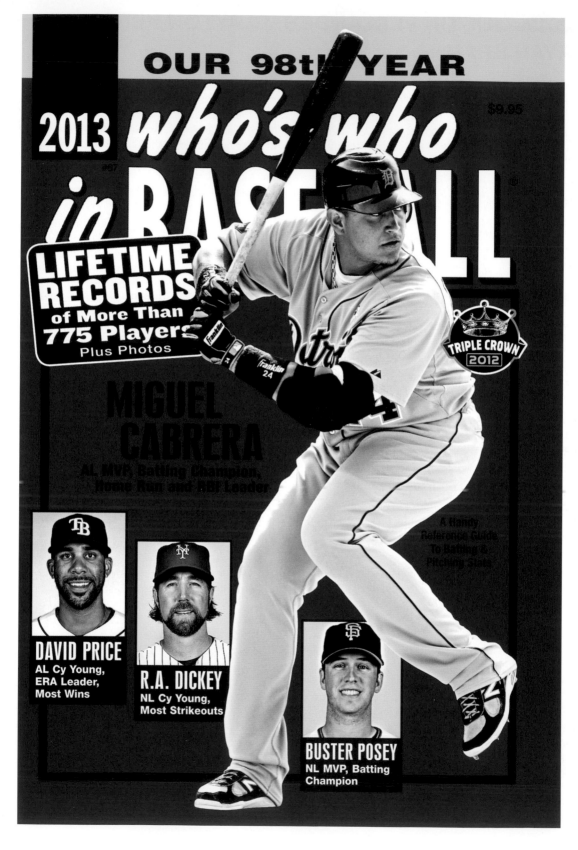

OUR 98th YEAR

$9.95

2013 who's who

#67

in BASEBALL

LIFETIME RECORDS
of More Than
775 Players
Plus Photos

TRIPLE CROWN
2012

MIGUEL CABRERA
AL MVP, Batting Champion,
Home Run and RBI Leader

A Handy
Reference Guide
To Batting &
Pitching Stats

DAVID PRICE
AL Cy Young,
ERA Leader,
Most Wins

R.A. DICKEY
NL Cy Young,
Most Strikeouts

BUSTER POSEY
NL MVP, Batting
Champion

2013—MIGUEL CABRERA, DAVID PRICE, R. A. DICKEY, BUSTER POSEY

In 2012, his 10th year in the majors, Miguel Cabrera became the first player in 46 years to win the Triple Crown—the last was Carl Yastrzemski in 1967—leading the American League in batting (.330), home runs (44), and RBIs (139).

During his career, Cabrera played third, first, outfield, and later DH. He was with the Florida Marlins from 2003 to 2007, and with the Detroit Tigers since 2008. While he had shown significant power in previous years, averaging about 30 homers and over 100 RBIs per season, he put it all together in 2012: He was also an All-Star, *The Sporting News* American League Player of the Year, and the AL Most Valuable Player, leading the Tigers to an 88-74 record and their 11th American League pennant, their first since 2006.

Cabrera led the AL in slugging percentage (.606), total bases (377), and extra base hits (84), and was second in runs scored (109) and hits (205)—altogether an absolute monster season.

Cabrera is under contract to the Tigers until at least 2025, when he will be 42.

David Price was the first Tampa Bay Ray to appear on the cover of *Who's Who in Baseball*. His best year was 2012, when he led the league with 20 wins, and with just five losses also led in won-loss percentage—.800, striking out 205 while walking just 59 batters in 211 innings, with a league-leading ERA of 2.56. Price also led the AL with seven shutouts. That record earned him a spot on the American League All-Star team and the AL Cy Young Award. Despite Price's outstanding season, the Rays finished third in the AL East.

R. A. (Robert Allen) Dickey was the only knuckleballer in the major leagues in 2012. He'd pitched for Texas, Seattle, and Minnesota, but really came into his own with the New York Mets (2010–2012). In 2012, he won the National League Cy Young Award and was an All-Star. His record was 20-6 with an ERA of 2.73 and an NL-leading 230 K's in 233.2 innings. After the 2012 season in which the Mets finished fourth in the AL East, Dickey was traded to the Toronto Blue Jays.

San Francisco Giants catcher Gerald Dempscy "Buster" Posey hit 24 home runs and led the majors with a .312 batting average on his way to the 2012 National League Most Valuable Player Award. He was also the NL's Comeback Player of the Year. (He played only 45 games in 2011.) Posey threw out a league-leading 38 attempted base-stealers.

In and Around Baseball 2012:

Starting in 2012, there were two wild card teams. Consequently, of the 30 major league teams, 10 made the postseason. Under the new system each league's two wild card teams played a one-game playoff, the winner to go to the Division Series. April 4: Muhammad Ali throws out the ceremonial first pitch as the Miami (neé Florida) Marlins play their first game at their new stadium, Marlins Park . . . April 21: Chicago White Sox pitcher Philip Humber's perfect game was his first complete game. Catcher A. J. Pierzynski dropped the final pitch of the game. As Brendan Ryan of the Seattle Mariners disputed the home plate umpire's strike three call, Pierzynski threw the ball to first base for the final out . . . May 8: Josh Hamilton of the Texas Rangers blasts four home runs and a double against the Baltimore Orioles for an AL record 18 total bases . . . June 1: Johan Santana throws the first no-hitter in New York Mets history . . . June 13: In the first perfect game in San Francisco Giants' history, Matt Cain becomes the first pitcher to score a run while pitching a perfect game. . . . August 3: B. J. Upton of the Tampa Bay Rays hits his 100th career home run. The same day, his brother Justin of the Arizona Diamondbacks hits *his* 100th career home run . . . August 15: Félix Hernández of the Seattle Mariners throws the third perfect game of 2012, beating the Tampa Bay Rays.

Buster Posey's leadership and prowess behind the plate and at bat (two homers and five RBIs in the Division Series, plus three RBIs in the Fall Classic) helped lead the Giants to a Series sweep over the Detroit Tigers in 2012.

OUR 99th YEAR

$2.95

2014 who's who in BASEBALL

LIFETIME RECORDS of More Than 775 Players
Plus Photos

CLAYTON KERSHAW
NL CY YOUNG, STRIKEOUT AND ERA LEADER

A Handy Reference Guide To Batting & Pitching Stats

ANDREW McCUTCHEN
NL MVP

MIGUEL CABRERA
AL MVP, Batting Champ

MAX SCHERZER
AL Cy Young, Most Wins

2014—CLAYTON KERSHAW, ANDREW MCCUTCHEN, MIGUEL CABRERA, MAX SCHERZER

Clayton Kershaw of the Los Angeles Dodgers was only 16-9 in 2013, but he led the National League with 232 strikeouts and had the lowest ERA in the NL (1.83) for the third year in a row. He was chosen for the All-Star team and won his second Cy Young Award.

Andrew McCutchen was the first Pittsburgh Pirate to appear on the cover of *Who's Who in Baseball* since Willie Stargell in 1980. He hit 21 home runs and stole 27 bases with 185 hits and 97 runs scored. Although he did not lead the National League in any major statistical category, he helped the Pirates to a 94-68 season—their first winning season since 1992. They were the NL Wild Card team in 2013, and McCutchen was chosen the Most Valuable Player in the National League.

In 2013, Miguel Cabrera of the Detroit Tigers followed up on his Triple Crown year in 2012 by hitting .348 and winning the American League batting crown for the third straight year. He won his second Most Valuable Player Award. He was also *The Sporting News* Major League Player of the Year again.

Max Scherzer of the Detroit Tigers had 21 wins, the most in the American League. He lost only three games, making his winning percentage .875, also tops in the AL. He was the AL Cy Young Award winner and *The Sporting News* American League Pitcher of the Year. Scherzer was the starting pitcher for the American League in the All-Star Game.

In and Around Baseball 2013:

After 51 years in the National League, the Houston Astros become just the second team (after the Milwaukee Brewers) to switch leagues: They join the American League West . . . August 5: Major League Baseball suspends a dozen players, the largest group ever, for using performance-enhancing drugs . . . September 20: Alex Rodriguez of the New York Yankees hits his 24th career grand slam, breaking Lou Gehrig's 77-year-old record of 23.

The Boston Red Sox win their third world championship of the 21st century, beating the St. Louis Cardinals 4–2. After going 86 years without a World Series win, the Red Sox have now won three in ten years.

OUR 100th YEAR

$9.95

2015 who's who
in BASEBALL®

LIFETIME
RECORDS
of More Than
775 Players
Plus Photos

MIKE
TROUT
AL MVP, RBI LEADER

COREY
KLUBER
AL Cy Young,
Most Wins

CLAYTON
KERSHAW
NL Cy Young,
MVP, Most Wins,
ERA Leader

A Handy
Reference Guide
To Batting
& Pitching Stats

2015—MIKE TROUT, COREY KLUBER, CLAYTON KERSHAW

22-year-old center fielder Mike Trout, a first-round draft pick of the Los Angeles Angels of Anaheim in 2009, was the Most Valuable Player in the American League—the first unanimous choice since Ken Griffey Jr. in 1997. Trout earned a Silver Slugger Award. He hit 36 home runs and batted .287 with 77 intentional walks. He led the AL with 111 RBIs, 115 runs scored, 338 total bases, and 84 extra base hits. He was also #1 in the AL with 184 strikeouts. The Angels won the AL West by 10 games but lost the Division Series to the Kansas City Royals.

The AL Cy Young Award went to Corey Kluber of the Cleveland Indians. He tied with Jered Weaver and Max Scherzer for first place in the American League with 18 wins, tied with six others with a league-leading 34 starts, was second with 269 strikeouts, and third with an ERA of 2.44.

Clayton Kershaw of the Los Angeles Dodgers won the National League Cy Young Award for 2014, his third in four years. He's the first pitcher ever to lead his league with the lowest ERA in four consecutive seasons. He was also named the league's MVP, the first pitcher to win both since Bob Gibson (National League) and Denny McClain (American League) each won both in 1968.

Kershaw led the Dodgers to the NL West title. Kershaw had the most wins in the NL (21), the lowest ERA (1.77), the best strikeout-to-walk ratio (7.710), and was third in strikeouts (239) to Stephen Strasburg and Johnny Cueto, tied at 242.

Kershaw was #1 in complete games (6), strikeouts per nine innings (10.845), winning percentage (.875), and third in shutouts (2-tied with six others).

New York Mets pitcher Jacob deGrom was the National League Rookie of the Year.

Chicago White Sox first baseman José Abreu was the American League Rookie of the Year.

In and Around Baseball 2014:

April 22: Albert Pujols of the Los Angeles Angels of Anaheim hits career home runs #499 and #500 in the same game—the first player to do so . . . June 18: Clayton Kershaw of the Dodgers does something that no pitcher has ever done before: He strikes out 15 Colorado Rockies while pitching a no-hitter . . . June 24: San Francisco Giants pitcher Tim Lincecum does something that hadn't been done in the major leagues for more than a century: He pitches his second no-hitter against the same team—the San Diego Padres. The last pitcher to no-hit the same team twice was Addie Joss of the Cleveland Indians, who blanked the Chicago White Sox in 1908 and 1910 . . . June 29: 5'6" José Altuve, nicknamed "Gigante," of the Houston Astros, does something that hadn't been done in 97 years, when Ray Chapman did it: He steals more than one base in four consecutive games . . . Altuve goes on to win the AL batting title with a .302 average while also leading the league in hits, singles, and stolen bases . . . July 13: For the first time ever, battery mates (San Francisco Giants pitcher Madison Bumgarner and catcher Buster Posey) both hit grand slams in the same game . . . September 28: Jordan Zimmerman of the Washington Nationals pitches a no-hitter on the last day of the season . . . Only one player in the American League hits 40 home runs—Nelson Cruz of the Baltimore Orioles—exactly 40. During the off season, Giancarlo Stanton of the Miami Marlins signs the richest contract in American Professional Sports—13 years for a total of $325,000,000. That's about $38,000 per at-bat.

World Series 2014:

The two teams in the 2014 World Series—the San Francisco Giants of the National League and the Kansas City Royals of the American—were both the Wild Card winners in their respective leagues. This is the first World Series for the Royals since they won in 1985. The Series goes to Game 7. Madison Bumgarner, pitching in relief of Jeremy Affeldt, retires 14 consecutive Royals and earns a save (to go with his two wins) as the Giants win the game 3-2 and the Series 4-3. "Mad Bum" is the Series MVP.

ACKNOWLEDGMENTS

Special thanks to the Baseball Hall of Fame, Pete Palmer, Marty Appel, Doug Lyons, Rita Halpern, Stanley Harris, Warren Sherman, Rory Slifkin, Stuart Shea, Scott Gould, Keith Wallman, Matt Rothenberg, Mark Arrow, Ben Harris, and all of baseball's fans and players.

ABOUT THE AUTHOR

Douglas B. Lyons is the author/coauthor of nine previous books about baseball. With his brother Jeffrey, he wrote three books of baseball trivia: *Out of Left Field, Curveballs and Screwballs,* and *Short Hops and Foul Tips.* He cowrote *Broadcast Rites and Sites* and *Can You Believe It?* with Red Sox broadcaster Joe Castiglione. He wrote *From an Orphan to a King* with Eddie Feigner of *The King and His Court,* and *Catching Heat* with Jeffrey Lyons and Jim Leyritz. On his own, he's the author of *Baseball: A Geek's Bible* and *Baseball: A Geek's Guide.* He is also the author of *American History: A Geek's Guide.*

A criminal lawyer, Mr. Lyons lives near New York City.

Pete Palmer is the co-author with John Thorn of *The Hidden Game of Baseball* and co-editor with Gary Gillette of the Barnes and Noble ESPN *Baseball Encyclopedia* (five editions). Pete introduced on-base average as an official statistic for the American League in 1979 and invented on-base plus slugging (OPS), now universally used as a good measure of batting strength. He was selected by the Society of American Baseball Research (SABR) in 2010 as a charter member for the Henry Chadwick Award. Pete also edited with John Thorn seven editions of *Total Baseball.* A member of SABR since 1973, Pete is also the editor of *Who's Who in Baseball,* which will celebrate its 100th year in 2015.